Hold My Watch

JOHNNY LEE COGBURN

WESTBOW
PRESS®
A DIVISION OF THOMAS NELSON
& ZONDERVAN

Copyright © 2021 Johnny Lee Cogburn.

All rights reserved. No part of this book may be used or reproduced by any means, graphic, electronic, or mechanical, including photocopying, recording, taping or by any information storage retrieval system without the written permission of the author except in the case of brief quotations embodied in critical articles and reviews.

This book is a work of non-fiction. Unless otherwise noted, the author and the publisher make no explicit guarantees as to the accuracy of the information contained in this book and in some cases, names of people and places have been altered to protect their privacy.

WestBow Press books may be ordered through booksellers or by contacting:

WestBow Press
A Division of Thomas Nelson & Zondervan
1663 Liberty Drive
Bloomington, IN 47403
www.westbowpress.com
844-714-3454

Because of the dynamic nature of the Internet, any web addresses or links contained in this book may have changed since publication and may no longer be valid. The views expressed in this work are solely those of the author and do not necessarily reflect the views of the publisher, and the publisher hereby disclaims any responsibility for them.

Any people depicted in stock imagery provided by Getty Images are models, and such images are being used for illustrative purposes only.
Certain stock imagery © Getty Images.

Scripture quotations taken from The Holy Bible, New International Version® NIV® Copyright © 1973 1978 1984 2011 by Biblica, Inc. TM. Used by permission. All rights reserved worldwide.

Scripture taken from the New King James Version® Copyright © 1982 by Thomas Nelson. Used by permission. All rights reserved.

Author photograph credit: Jeremy Cowart
Myra Belle Baugh

ISBN: 978-1-6642-4172-5 (sc)
ISBN: 978-1-6642-4174-9 (hc)
ISBN: 978-1-6642-4173-2 (e)

Library of Congress Control Number: 2021915197

Print information available on the last page.

WestBow Press rev. date: 08/12/2021

This book is dedicated to my lovely wife, Marilyn.

(Illustration by Myra Baugh)

Contents

Preface ix

Marilyn 1

Johnny 10

School Years 45

Marilyn and Johnny 63

Teaching and Coaching Years 83

Retirement and "the Retirement House" 109

Forgetfulness and Change 131

The Move, and Life in Fayetteville 144

At the Attorney's Office in Danville 150

The Day-to-Day Struggle with Change and Loneliness 157

Our Testimony 192

Reflections 198

The End of Our Life Journey 211

About the Author 219

Preface

My prayer was answered when Marilyn Kay Patterson from Danville, Arkansas, traveled to the school gym in Magazine, Arkansas, with her sister to meet the newly hired coach from Texas. Since 1968 I had been praying to find someone with similar values, someone who believes God is the creator of the universe and that mankind can be saved through his son, Jesus. This was the spiritual connection I prayed for many nights before going to bed. When I met Marilyn for the first time, I knew my prayers had been answered.

Although we were raised in God-fearing homes, our childhood and adolescent years were different. Yet above all else, we shared a commitment to serving God. Our professional careers were just getting started. Our temperaments and personalities were compatible. We lived and dreamed of our retirement years.

Then Alzheimer's brought about a separation that changed our lives after forty-eight years of marriage. The love, happiness, and joy we shared gave way to an incurable illness that caused feelings of sadness, rejection, heartache, and loneliness. The disease sent us on a downward path filled with inward pain and grief. It forced us to make the hard decision to sell our home—a home built for our retirement—and move closer to our daughters for help with long-term care. We had anxiety about moving in our autumn years to a new location because we were uncertain about whether we would like the city.

This is our journey of love that continued to grow spiritually in lives filled with devotion to God, family, and each other.

Marilyn

Marilyn was born in the local clinic in Danville, Arkansas, on August 30, 1948. She was a resident of Danville through her college years. Marilyn's family was one of many whose lives centered around family, church, school, and their jobs. Danville is a typical rural town located in a valley, with a mountain range that borders the city on the south and the Petit Jean River that runs through the edge of town to the north. The mountains to the south make for a scenic backdrop, especially when snow covers them in winter. In the spring, the blooms of the dogwood trees are so attractive.

The strength of Danville's economy comes from its people, who work in chicken growing, chicken plant processing, farming, cattle ranching, and the forest industries. They work in schools, banks, at the phone company, for the county government, and at the hospital.

Marilyn's mother, Ruth, worked at the hospital in Danville as a nurse for thirty-five years. She helped deliver many babies in the county, including two of our daughters, Shelly and Leslie. Marilyn's father, Jimmy, worked for the county maintaining roads. Later, before retiring, he was employed by the local phone company.

After completing his military service in the 1940s, Jimmy played American Legion baseball on a team in Danville with other men of the town who had completed their hitch with Uncle Sam. They were all good players. It was my understanding their team was quite good. Jimmy was also an avid St. Louis Cardinals baseball fan, whose games he enjoyed watching after church on Sundays. Nothing else really mattered at the time.

Marilyn's house was the "community playground," with her five siblings at home plus other friends who walked to her house after school to play basketball and touch football. All were in serious competition with each other, but they all played for fun.

Marilyn loved school, along with all the activities it had to offer. She played the clarinet, marched in the band, was a cheerleader, ran track, and played softball. She loved the competition of all sports and was a good athlete. Basketball was her favorite. She lettered in both junior and senior years. Her family members, like Marilyn, were sports-minded. Her siblings were all good athletes as well and played for the Little Johns.

Marilyn's mother, Ruth, worked the night shift at the Danville hospital, but before she left for work, she always made those melt-in-your-mouth chocolate chip cookies for Marilyn and her friends when they came home from school. Ruth passed along to Marilyn caring, sharing, and humbleness of mind. I saw those traits in Marilyn when I fell in love with her.

According to one of Marilyn's lifelong friends, who was also her classmate, when Marilyn was in fourth grade, she and her friends had a club. The membership was by invitation only. After school, the members met in an old shed one block from Marilyn's house in town. The purpose of this exclusive club—whose members were sworn to secrecy—was to discuss who was dating whom. These were important discussions to students in fourth grade.

Going to the movies in Danville was much fun. The theater, located on Main Street, was in walking distance of Marilyn's house. She and her friends took many trips upstairs to the bathroom—not necessarily to use the bathroom but to check out the so-called "love birds" in the balcony.

After the movie, Marilyn walked her friend home. Then her friend walked Marilyn home, and then her friend had to walk home alone.

On occasion, after school was out, Marilyn and her friends walked to the local soda fountain in the drug store on Front Street. Marilyn always ordered an RC Cola in a bottle and a package of peanuts. She then stuffed that bottle full of peanuts.

In the late 1950s, Danville was hit by a big snowstorm. School was closed. Marilyn and her friends wished they had a sled to join the other students sledding down the steep hill on the street behind the courthouse. She and her friends decided to borrow the door off her father's doghouse. They had a blast sliding down that steep hill. However, the fun ended when Marilyn's father realized the door was missing from his doghouse. Now Marilyn was *in the doghouse.*

The Yell County Fair was a big event each September. The Friday of that week was designated as a school holiday. The day started with the parade of marching bands, floats, and students carrying their school's banner with pride. Marilyn marched in the parade with the Danville High School Band while playing the clarinet. After the parade, she worked with her classmates in a booth to raise money for their class projects. She also enjoyed the rides the fair had to offer, riding them with her friends.

Like many other towns of its size, Danville looked forward to football season. The businesses in town were always supportive of the Little Johns, the school mascot, with all types of weekly pregame activities, such as signs in business windows, banners stretched across the street at intersections, and parades celebrating homecoming. These activities led up to the big Friday night games. During deer season, hunters left their camps on Friday evening to line up along the chain-link fence around the football field in support of the Little Johns.

Recreational activities have always been part of the community because of the close proximity to rivers, lakes, and state parks, all offering a variety of leisure-time fun a few miles away. Hunting and fishing was how many spent their spare time. Marilyn's father was either fishing for bass or hunting for quail, duck, rabbit, squirrel, deer, or turkey, whatever was in season.

When wild game was brought home, her father, Jimmy, cleaned it and prepped it for cooking. Marilyn's mother and grandmother were great cooks and knew many ways to prepare game. But since her mom worked long hours as a nurse, her grandmother took on the majority of the cooking. Each day, the meal of wild game or fish would be cooked and on the table by noon. The expected friends and relatives dropped in after hunting or fishing and knew there would be plenty of food and conversation. The conversation was usually about the great Razorback games of the past, as well as the fishing or hunting stories of the day, followed with sympathetic laughter—especially over the one that got away.

On Sunday afternoons during the summer, Jimmy routinely took Marilyn, her siblings, and friends swimming. They loaded up in the back of his pickup and headed to Spring Lake, a state park not far from Danville. Small towns often lend themselves toward good-natured mischief. On this particular Sunday afternoon, when the baseball game was over, a young teenaged Marilyn and one of her close friends decided to partake in this pastime. The swimming area at the park was roped off. Swimming outside this protective area was against park rules, but they made their own rules. Marilyn and her friend pretended that the whole lake was part of the roped-off area so they could swim wherever they liked. Marilyn's father, however, was not impressed with their Olympic-style swim across the lake near the dam area and back.

Marilyn was an excellent swimmer. During the summers

of her high school years, she worked as a lifeguard at the city pool. After completing her shifts, she and her friends played tennis at the city park.

Marilyn's older sister told me a story that happened in June 1959. After the long school year had ended, she and Marilyn, both in their teens, decided to accept an invitation from their aunt, uncle, and cousin, who lived in New Orleans, to come for a visit. They boarded a train in Danville, had a brief layover in Shreveport, boarded another train, and arrived at their destination in New Orleans. This cousin was on a softball team and played games at night. Marilyn and her sister went to games in support of their cousin. During the day they all went downtown to the French Quarter to observe how the French lived, try new foods, and listen to the spoken language. This trip to the French Quarter may have had an influence on Marilyn to study French in college as a second language. When their visit was over, they boarded a train and returned to Danville. What a trip for two teenaged sisters that has long been remembered!

In May of 1966, graduation day had finally arrived. Marilyn had achieved the acclaim of being in the National Honor Society in junior high and high school. She was appreciative of all her teachers, but one, her high school English teacher, Catherine Rogers, had an influence on her to pursue a career in education.

After graduation, Marilyn attended Ouachita Baptist University in Arkadelphia for one year and then transferred to Arkansas Tech University in the fall of 1967 to continue her studies. There, she moved into a dorm across the street from What-a-Burger Restaurant. She and her friends spent much time between classes not only eating burgers and fries but discussing what every other college girl probably discusses—the cutest boys on campus. In her first year of studies at Arkansas Tech, she made the dean's list.

After graduating in May 1970, she moved back in with her parents in Danville and was living with them when she began teaching English at Havana High School.

Johnny

My hometown of Bagwell, Texas, was not as picturesque as Marilyn's. There were no local lakes or mountains. It had piney woods and hardwood timber on flat terrain with sandy loam and black soil. Bagwell was an unincorporated town located in the northeast corner of the state. It boasted a population of fewer than two hundred in the 1950s. Without city services, the water supply came from hand-dug wells, stock ponds, and rainwater that was funneled from the eaves of houses into galvanized tanks.

All houses had a bathroom. The only problem was that the bathroom was not inside the house. The outhouse, as it was called in those days, was located well behind the house. Because of its location, snakes were a common concern, especially at night when walking the trodden paths. The outhouses were always furnished with Sears Roebucks catalogues in case someone wanted to place an order or follow the latest trends. They were also used for other things when needed.

In the late 1940s and early '50s, the town consisted of a post office, three gas station convenience stores, a café, an auto repair shop, and a blacksmith's shop that doubled as a domino parlor. It also had three churches, a school, and a big cottonwood tree. This cottonwood tree, known as the "the tree," joined the walkway in front of the stores on one side of the street. "The tree" was at least three feet in diameter and approximately 120 years old. Because of its size, the roots protruded above the ground level, and people sat on its roots. Young and old gathered under its shade telling stories from the past and present.

On the east side of "the tree" was a hitching rail. It was not uncommon to see a rancher who had been working cattle or locating a stray calf or cow, ride up, tie his horse, and go into the store or blacksmith shop for business or to the café for food. It was a rendezvous place where people met to visit or just hang out, waiting for a farmer to come by who needed help hauling hay or a rancher who needed help working cattle. People from far and wide knew the location of "the tree."

Three miles north of Bagwell is where my parents, Loney and Olevia Cogburn, made their home. In 1946, Olevia was pregnant. They stepped out of their log house and into a 1929 Model A Ford and traveled ten miles to the hospital in Clarksville so she could give birth. At 6:45 a.m. on Tuesday, October 29, 1946, Olevia gave birth to a son they named Johnny Lee.

The following year, in May, after my oldest brother graduated from eighth grade, my parents loaded up their four sons, Buddy (age fourteen), Benny (twelve), Gene (ten), and eight-month-old Johnny Lee into their Model A Ford to begin their trip to California to look for employment.

Johnny Lee Cogburn being held by his half-sister, Lucille, November 1946 (Photo from family album, Olevia Cogburn).

When we arrived in California, my parents searched for work in the cotton fields, walnut groves, peach orchards, and grape vineyards. The path was the same as migrant workers before us who came in search for a better quality of life for their families. This was the last of three trips like this as a family. We usually stayed from nine to eighteen months each time. During our stays, we lived in different cities, which were within a short driving distance of the San Joaquin Valley.

My father got acquainted with Mike, the owner of a grape

vineyard. During the harvest season, a lot of our time was spent at his vineyard.

Grape vineyard in San Joaquin Valley, California. (Illustration by Myra Baugh)

When we left California for the last time in December 1949, I was three years old. Even though I was very young, the image of those Thompson seedless grapes hanging on the vines in clusters is vivid to this day. After we completed our employment for the year, my parents decided to move back to Texas, and we lived in Dallas until August 1951. Then we moved to Bagwell. I was five years old and not old enough under Texas law to start school.

My mother leased the local café and we lived in the rear, and there was not much for a five-year-old to do. However, there were plenty of educational opportunities for me under "the tree." For example, the local high school dropouts were good role models. They offered guidance and advice to young minds willing to listen. Then there was the domino parlor inside the blacksmith shop next door. It was an excellent source for the advancement of a young lad's education. With the old men and their obscene jokes, a five-year-old had a head start in his education before he reached first grade.

The Whiskey Tree. (Illustration by Myra Baugh)

The local moonshine pick-up place was known by all in the community as the "whisky tree." The location was about one mile north of town. To place an order for the 120-proof freshly brewed corn liquor, the two parties prearranged a time for the delivery of the money and the product. With the arrangement in place, the customer went to the tree, left money at the base, and then drove a little way down the road. This allowed the person making the delivery time to go to the tree, pick up the money, set the quart-sized fruit jar at the base of the tree, and leave. The buyer and seller may have passed each other on the road, but no personal contact was made. When all was clear, the customer would pick up the product by the "whisky tree," which stood one hundred-plus years and represented a way of life for those who exchanged goods under cover of its shade.

The town has always been a private community of hardworking people who mostly made their living in the logging industry, as chicken growers, ranchers, or row crop farmers. There were other businesses whose location was kept undisclosed and known only by a few for obvious reasons.

The local law enforcement officer, the county sheriff, was eight miles away. For these businesses, this was for the best. The politics of the day was that their lives were better with less government involvement.

The only thing to do in town after six o'clock was to gather at the base of "the tree" to talk, throw rocks, and watch the caution light at the intersection as it blinked away time. I sometimes used my watch to count the number of times the light blinked in one minute. I did that just to have something to do. The reason was all businesses in town closed at six; some even closed earlier.

We boys threw rocks at railroad cars waiting to be loaded the next day with cargo. The distance from "the tree" to the boxcars on the tracks was between 100 and 125 yards. The challenge for the thrower was to find a rock not too heavy and not too light, but one with sailing qualities. Even the best thrower could not reach that distance with any rock. Each of us took turns throwing. After throwing the rocks, we had to wait a few seconds to hear that clinging sound as it reached its destination. This rock-throwing contest was the highlight of the evening.

The café was one of the main businesses in town. This was where many of the locals came to eat, visit, and catch up on the latest news or gossip. Visitors passing through on Highway 82, the main highway from Texarkana and Dallas, often stopped to eat and play the jukebox. One popular song in 1951, sung by Hank Williams, was "Hey, Good Lookin'." The song could be heard through the open windows of the café by those playing dominoes inside the open-air blacksmith shop located next door.

The café my mother ran was a good source of income for our family. In the spring of 1952, my dad and Uncle Burl Hasting began building our future home on the forty acres of land my parents purchased with the money they saved working in California. After the house was completed, we moved from the rear of the café into our new home. However, my mother continued to run the café. This was the start of a more normal family environment for me. At the time we finished building, we did not have the required $800 for the electric company to run service to our house from the closest neighbor's house a half mile away.

Although we didn't have electricity, we moved into our house around the middle of August. It was so hot at night we couldn't sleep, so my parents decided we would sleep outside on cots under the stars. I can still visualize the beauty of the sky full of stars. By September, the nights got cooler, and we were able to sleep inside more comfortably.

During the summer of 1952, I was in my mother's café when a huge bus stopped in front of the gas station across the street. Curious about who could possibly be on that bus and why they would be stopping in Bagwell, I crossed the street and stood at the open door of the bus. Though it seemed empty, when I looked up, there in the front seat was a man wearing a western-style hat. He had his boots propped up on the handrail at the entrance of the bus with a cigar in his mouth, waiting for the others to return from the convenience store with the food they had purchased.

He looked at me and said, "Howdy."

I said, "Howdy," back.

On the side of the bus, near the top, was written "Bob Wills and his Texas Playboys."

The day Bob Wills and his Texas Playboys stopped in Bagwell. (Illustration by Myra Baugh)

After Bob and "the Boys" left town, I tried to imagine what it would be like to travel on that fine tour bus with my name, Johnny Lee, on the side while reading my favorite comic book with a prime cigar resting between my lips and blowing smoke rings out of my mouth.

I wanted to be like Bob, so I headed back to my mother's café and made my way behind the counter to the display case where those handsome King Edward cigars were located. I sneaked one out of the case and headed straight for the outhouse. Once inside, I shut the door and sat down. I could hardly wait to fire up that long stogie! After firing up that stick, I reached for the Sears catalogue, looking for the toy section. While dreaming of relaxing on one of those fine, soft, colored seats traveling along Highway 82 heading for the big city of Dallas, the smoke rolled out through the halfmoon vent over the door.

The outhouse, the bathroom of the day.
(Illustration by Myra Baugh)

After a few puffs, my daydreaming left me rather quickly. King Edward and I began to have some issues. I decided we were no longer friends. I got up, laid the catalog down, deposited the king, and bid him farewell. I had trouble opening the draggy door to the outhouse. Why was this happening to me? I could not expect any sympathy from my mother because I knew none would be given. The rest of my day was not pleasant, to say the least.

On Tuesday, September 1, 1953, the first day of school finally arrived. I had already begun my worldly education; now it was time for my formal education. I entered Mrs. Effie Henry's first grade classroom. I was looking forward to learning reading, writing, and arithmetic plus enjoy the excitement of recess and lunch. I could hardly wait!

There was no cafeteria. We carried our lunches in paper bags or lunch pails. My mother always packed a wholesome lunch for me. It consisted of a smoked ham sandwich from the smokehouse on our farm, cookies, fruit (whatever kind was available), and milk brought in my thermos. My jeans and shirts were always starched and ironed. What a wonderful mother!

One day, a friend asked if I wanted to swap lunches. He had bologna but wanted my ham sandwich. I agreed. Looking back, I do not believe I got the fair end of that swap.

At recess, the name of the game was King of the Hill. At the back of the school was a pond that supplied water for the school. Half the bank was fenced off. The other half was a hill used for play. The idea was to stay on top of the hill for as long as you could without others dragging you off by the arms, feet, body, clothes, or whatever they could get their hands on. The game was a test of strength, endurance, and the will to determine who would be king. There was no announcement of a winner. Everyone's clothes were dirty. If it rained, the red clay mud covered my starched and ironed jeans. I would get a stick and rake the mud off the best I could before going home.

My mother's response was, "What in the world have you been doing?"

I still remember sitting at the kitchen table eating dinner, my father speaking words of appreciation for Mike, the owner of the grape vineyard in California, for the employment he provided our family.

After the table was cleared, my mother helped me with my schoolwork by the light of a coal oil lamp. After a time we would take a break, and Mother brought me a cookie and a glass of milk. When my assignments were completed, we moved closer to the fireplace for the warmth it provided, being the only means of heat in our home. Then she would open her Bible and read me stories, such as Moses in the bulrushes, Joseph and his coat of many colors, and baby Jesus born in a manger. My mother was not only helping me with my formal education but to find purpose in life. She helped lay a foundation for my spiritual walk with God. She wanted to do as much as possible in her lifetime to prepare not only me but her entire family for a spiritual life that would lead to eternal salvation.

Mother found spiritual purpose in her life as a restaurant employee and café owner. She was well known throughout the community as an excellent baker and cook, setting the bar for others. She also gave much of her time back to the community in preparing and delivering food to those who lost loved ones, the shut-ins, the disabled, and our friends and neighbors who were ill for a period of time and couldn't work. Mother gave far more in her lifetime to others than she received herself.

For a farm boy who lived two miles north of town with the closest neighbor half a mile away, there were some days the only person I would see, other than my family, was the rural mail carrier. Many times, while mowing our half acre yard, I saw him coming in the distance. I would stop my push mower and run to get the mail before he left, just to talk to him about his son, who was a close friend.

After chores, if any spare time was left, I spent it fishing in the stock pond behind our house. My mother's voice can still be heard calling, "Johnny Lee-eee!" to come home for lunch or dinner. She only had to call for me once because I was always hungry. This was an appreciation for a simpler time in my life when a cane pole, line, hook, cork, and worms or grasshoppers (if I could catch them) filled the gaps between chores.

First day of squirrel season. Ready!
(Photo from Cogburn family album)

The beginning of squirrel hunting season was October 2, 1954, a Saturday. My uncle Burl came to our farm ready to hunt and asked if I wanted to go with him. After getting permission from my parents, we left in his wagon pulled by a team of horses with my new squirrel hunting dog my dad had bought for me.

Every boy needs a dog. I was so proud of my black and tan hound named Joe. He was an excellent squirrel dog. He would circle the wagon in about a one hundred-yard radius. If he did not tree a squirrel he would come back, and we kept moving.

This process kept us busy all day long, and by the time we got home, we had about twenty squirrels to clean and prepare. Squirrel and dumplings with homemade biscuits, creamed potatoes, and gravy were on the menu that night!

Also in 1954 on a cool Halloween evening, my mother took a couple of friends and me trick-or-treating. We had made our masks out of paper bags. Back then, we did not have access to much candy, so any type of treats were appreciated. The next morning, when Mother took me to school, we passed through the town and noticed that there was a car on top of a building. This was a very strange sight to say the least, an obvious Halloween prank. To get that car on top of that flat roof took much effort. It was customary to expect something extremely unusual to occur on Halloween night in Bagwell each year.

Thanksgiving and Christmas holidays were fast approaching. By this time, we had paid the electric company the required amount to install electricity in our home, which was helpful for my mother since she always spent much time preparing food and planning for the holidays.

Preparations started at least two or three weeks in advance. This was our usual time frame to begin looking for a Christmas tree. My father and I started the search on Saturday morning after breakfast. Using propane gas that supplied our cookstove, Mother fixed a breakfast of farm sausage, country ham, streak gravy made straight from the grease, fresh eggs, and homemade biscuits to be topped with butter churned by me the day before, and muscadine jelly and sorghum molasses to fit inside those biscuits. What a breakfast!

After we found that perfect tree, Mother and I would decorate. Then it was time for Mother to begin making the date loaf and divinity and fudge candies. These were always the first to be made and a portion of these holiday treats were packaged for shipping to her sons, Gene and Buddy, on battleships stationed overseas. The other portion would be placed in the freezer. Then she would make Italian cream cake followed with a made-from-scratch fruitcake. These would also be placed in the freezer.

Two days before the holidays, whether Thanksgiving or

Christmas, she made two sweet potato pies along with apple, raisin, and apricot. Next she made coconut and chocolate pies, which were placed in the refrigerator overnight to be ready for the meringue topping the next morning. I must not overlook those apple and apricot fried pies, which were prepared a couple of days prior to the big day.

Mother's biggest challenge was to keep her baby son's hands away from those fried apricot pies, which were my favorite. What a cook and mother!

In the spring of 1955 I went with my father to the First National Bank in Clarksville, Texas, with the intention of obtaining a loan for $150. This was a memorable banking experience for an eight-year-old boy. We met with a loan officer my father knew and had done business with many times in the past. We planned to purchase weaning calves, which in those days could be purchased at market value for around $15 per head. The loan would buy about ten head, which we would bottle feed until they were fully able to feed themselves. We kept them about six months or until the fall and sold them at market price, which was considerably more than the initial cost.

What I am about to describe is a banking practice that does not exist anymore. My father shook hands with the banker and explained the nature of his business. The banker asked how much money my father needed and how he planned to pay back the loan. My father explained his plan and how the loan would be paid back within six months. The banker went back to the safe and brought back with him the $150 we needed for the loan. What was so unique about this transaction was that there was no bank note to sign. There was only a verbal agreement between two men followed by a handshake that sealed the agreement.

By summer 1955, I had a job mowing the lawn of one of the store owners. My father helped me transport the lawn mower back and forth. I earned one dollar and twenty-five cents for about forty-five minutes of work. To an eight-year-old boy, that was a lot of money. This mowing project was set up for every two weeks. This was a great opportunity for me to earn spending money. After a few weeks of mowing, the blade became dull and needed sharpening. So I pushed my mower to the local mechanic shop where they sharpened blades and asked the mechanic how much it would cost to sharpen mine.

He told me, "If you take off the blade, I'll charge you fifty cents, but if I take off the blade, it will be one dollar."

Being a good businessman and wanting to protect my hard-earned cash, I decided to take the blade off myself and save the fifty cents. I asked him if I could borrow a wrench to take it off.

He said, "Ok."

As I began to take the blade off, the wrench slipped, and the blade sliced the top of my hand open. The blood started to flow. As I stood there in pain with tears streaming down my face, the mechanic came up to me. I expected him to help and offer comfort, but when I looked up at him with my tear-streaked face, he leaned down and said, "Now you see what the other fifty cents is for." That was one lesson I learned in Bagwell, Texas, but it cost skin and blood.

Auto repair shop; mower blades sharpened here.
(Illustration by Myra Baugh)

Another lesson occurred in 1957, when I entered the fifth grade. The school had just installed a new merry-go-round. It was so much fun to see how fast we boys could push it around to make the girls scream. The louder they screamed, the faster we pushed. One day when the bell rang signaling it was time to go to class, a couple of boys and I decided to see how fast we could make it turn. The second bell rang, and we jumped off. When I jumped, one of the bolts hooked the seat of my pants and ripped the seam out of the rear! I immediately grabbed my rear and went to class holding my pants shut.

The teacher asked, "What's wrong, Johnny?"

You cannot imagine the laughter and how loud it was! The teacher got some safety pins and pinned the rear of my pants back together. My face turned as red as the paint on the new merry-go-round. Later, as an adult, my wife and I took our daughter Shelly there when she was three. We took a picture of her on that same merry-go-round. The school is no longer there, but the memories remain.

Shelly on the merry-go-round where my pants were ripped.
(Photo from Cogburn family album)

While my mother ran the local café, my father got into the business of raising chickens for Pilgrim's Pride on our forty-acre farm. For a young boy, there was much to do on the family farm. I helped feed the chickens and cleaned out the chicken house after a batch was raised and sold. I also helped feed the cows and hogs, plant the garden, and harvest the five-acre truck patch. It was full of corn, sweet potatoes, and watermelons, plus the small half-acre garden that was full of purple hull peas, crowder peas, okra, and onions. We loaded the vegetables and watermelons into the truck and drove into town to sell our produce by the side of Highway 82 (hence the "truck patch"). I also helped build the fences. The post holes were all dug by hand, especially mine. My father measured the holes. They all had to be at least two feet deep.

On Saturday evenings, after the work was finished and dinner was eaten, we gathered around the battery-operated radio to listen to the Grand Ole Opry broadcast on WSM from Nashville featuring Roy Acuff. He usually sang two of his greatest hits, "Wabash Cannonball" and "Great Speckled Bird."

On many occasions, friends were invited to our home to play dominoes or forty-two. Mother would always have sandwiches, candy, cookies, coffee, and soft drinks. My father also enjoyed baking sweet potatoes in a Dutch oven over the coals in our fireplace for our guests. There were other times we popped popcorn in a metal pan over the fire in the fireplace.

In the early-to-mid 1950s, my brothers served our country. Gene was in the navy while Buddy, the oldest, served in the air force. Like my parents, I always looked forward to them coming home on furloughs. Mother prepared that special meal or birthday celebration that they missed while serving our country. They would tell stories of those faraway places they had seen in their travels, places that I could only imagine or read about in books. They were simple yet happy times for our family.

My parents placed church involvement as a priority, not only following Christian principles in their lives but also by example to their family. All the years with my parents, I cannot remember a Sunday where we did not attend church as a family.

On many occasions we invited the visiting minister to our home for the usual dinner of fried chicken, purple hull peas, sweet corn, mashed potatoes, gravy, and a tomato plate with cucumbers, sweet peppers, and onions. Homemade yeast rolls were prepared and left to rise on the stovetop ready for baking after church. Mother had two pies for dessert: one chocolate and one coconut. Prepping for the main course of the meal was started by six o'clock in the morning and was ready before we left for church. After church, the final touches were put on the meal, and we would be ready to eat by one o'clock. We sat at the table, and the visiting minister would give thanks. Mother served dessert on the china plates my brother Gene sent to her from Japan while he was in the navy. The Sunday meal was always enjoyed by all.

These years on the farm, 1952 to 1959, molded my character. My father was instrumental in teaching me how to be innovative, self-reliant, and independent. Loney Clark Cogburn passed along stories to me about life and how it was lived in the late 1800s. He told me stories that his father told him. His father, my grandfather, fought in the Civil War and told of outlaw gangs riding on horseback to my grandparents' house. My grandfather went to the door to see what they wanted. The men never dismounted. In that day and time, it was a show of courtesy and respect to stay on one's horse until invited to step down. This was especially true of private farms and homes. They said they were hungry and needed a meal, for which they offered to pay. My grandmother prepared them a meal. They were polite, and when finished, they placed their money on the kitchen table and left.

I had many conversations with my father about how he lived in both the nineteenth and twentieth centuries. He turned sixteen at the beginning of the twentieth century. Although our conversation spanned into two centuries at different times, his thoughts seemed to drift to the years of the 1930s more than any other. He talked about how hard it was finding jobs to make a living during those years, the Depression years. He explained there were simply not enough jobs to employ the amount of people who were seeking employment.

Those were the years that people had little to no money. On March 4, 1929, President Herbert Hoover was sworn in as the thirty-first president of the United States. He ran on the slogan "A chicken in every pot and a car in every garage." Seven months after he was sworn in, the financial market crashed in October 1929, ushering in the Great Depression, which lasted until 1939. The president's slogan did not come true. Families were devastated.

Those Depression years my father lived through were the years he, as well as others of that generation, put to use and relied on concepts taught to them by their pioneer parents. Nature and its surrounding resources played a big part in their survival on a day-to-day basis. They were not worried about next week's food supply. Putting food on the table today was the priority.

I was told of a technique those pioneers used to find beehives deep in the forest, called bee coursing. They would first put out bait like watermelon, cantaloupe, or peaches that would attract bees. Then they would place a speck of flour on one bee and observe its flight direction, accounting for the time it took to return to the hive from the bait. Each time the bee left the bait, the pioneers shortened the distance between the bait and the hive, all the while calculating the distance and time. Those who used the technology of the day and followed the bees into the forest were rewarded with their winter supply of honey.

One simple lesson in economics taught to me by my father at a young age has never been forgotten, and it is one that I have drawn from all my life. Keep in mind, he lived through those Depression years of the 1930s. The lesson was this: if I have spare time and have no money and someone offers me fifty cents to do a job, and for some reason I turned down the offer, the opportunity to earn wages and put my extra time to use has been lost. I may have other offers in the future, but the one I just turned down will not be available again, and I am still broke with nothing but my spare time. I have used this concept all my life to take jobs others would not take because they thought their time was more valuable. I would take the job, put my time to use, and accept the wages.

One story was told to me by a good friend who lived through those Depression years in Arkansas. His story was from his teen years when he lived at home with his mom, dad, and younger siblings. The family had no meat to eat at the time. Hunting was the best and easiest way to provide meat for the family. It was winter, and there happened to be a big snowfall the night before. He told his mom and dad he was going hunting since they had not had any meat to eat in several days. So he got his .22 rifle and headed out to find any type of game that he could find. The first game tracks he came across were made by a rabbit. This would be a good start if he could only follow those tracks long enough to get a shot at the rabbit. After following the tracks for a distance, he told me someone else had gotten in front of him and started tracking the same rabbit. This was not good, so he turned around and left the area to go in the opposite direction to see what else he could find.

He came upon another set of rabbit tracks a long way from the first set. He followed those tracks. After tracking for a distance, lo and behold he came across another set of human tracks just ahead. This was how competitive hunting game for food in rural Arkansas was in those Depression years of the 1930s. He gave up on finding any game that day and headed back home. He had to forge a creek between him and his house. He looked down in the creek and there was a huge, soft-shelled turtle. He didn't know why a turtle would be in that location in shallow water during the cold of winter.

He said, "We had meat for a few days thanks to that soft-shelled turtle!"

The past generations who lived in rural America during the Depression had large families to work the family farm. They were self-sustaining people who relied on their families, neighbors, and friends. They bartered among themselves with their time and labor. Hunting, fishing, trapping, and farming were their ways of survival. It was a way of life that has long been forgotten in today's world where the next meal is only a phone call away and delivered to your door within minutes.

My father, Loney Clark Cogburn. (Photo from Cogburn family album)

My father's horse was the main mode of transportation. Horses could be ridden or used to pull buggies and wagons. Then he saw the production of the Model T invented by Henry Ford on October 1, 1908.

My father lived during World War I. He worked as a deputy marshal and drove a school bus in Stewart, Oklahoma, in the 1930s. He experienced the hardships of the Great Depression and the Dust Bowl. My father saw men go to the moon in 1969 and lived a lifetime of change. He was able to make a living and adapt to all the changes he experienced. My father was born on December 29, 1884, and passed this life as a Christian on July 20, 1971.

Through church attendance, Bible study, and the examples both parents set as Christians, my spiritual walk took root. My mother spent much time reading Bible stories to me as a child. Then in my teen years, my faith had guided me to a belief in Christ as the Son of God. This was the motivating force that caused my obedience to the Gospel of Christ. I studied scripture to get a better understanding of how the first century Christians obeyed the gospel, what the gospel was, and its meaning. My search led me to 1 Corinthians 15:1-4. By understanding this scripture and how it applied to Romans 6:3-6 helped me understand my conversion to Christ and the meaning of the gospel. My obedience to the Gospel of Christ set the course for my life with God's word as my guide. The conversions set forth by those early Christians recorded throughout the apostles' letters were the examples I wanted to follow in my conversion. My spiritual walk has taken many detours off the tried-and-true path but never far from my roots. Prayer and forgiveness have always been part of my faith.

School Years

One of our closest neighbors was a black family. Their son was my age and went to the segregated school. In late summer of 1958, just before school started, I rode my bike to town. On my way home, I passed their house. He was playing basketball. I stopped and we visited a bit. He asked if I wanted to shoot hoops. I accepted but could not stay long because my parents were expecting me home to finish my chores before dark. After a few minutes of shooting baskets, I thanked him for letting me play and asked if I could come back and play another day. He said yes. This was the start of a friendship that began with two kids playing basketball. This was how we spent some of our free time as kids two miles north of town. Even though we were of different races, playing together shaped my character and laid the foundation during these formative years that had a lasting effect on my future career as a public school teacher and coach.

I entered sixth grade in September 1958. That year, the school put up new basketball goals, and I spent recess time shooting hoops. My friend, Louis Nolan, had introduced me to the sport a few weeks earlier. I asked my parents to put up a goal at home and they did, mounted on a tree not far from our house. Although I had a new goal, my chores after school took up much of the daylight time. By the time I was finished it was dark, and we did not have outside lights. So if I wanted to shoot hoops, it would have to be after dark. The problem this created was not being able to see the ball and not knowing if the ball went through the hoop. That was when sound started playing a role in communicating to me when a basket was made. I heard a distinct swishing sound. Little did I know at the time that the feel of the ball, the follow-through of motion, and hearing a basket being made was developing my shooting skills in the dark of night.

In 1958, about two weeks before Christmas, the teacher sent me and a couple of my friends to find a tree. We wandered down to the creek under the railroad tracks to get to one of my friend's grandparents' house. We were really looking for something to eat. His grandmother gave us some food and then we continued to search for a tree. We finally found one and returned to the school around two o'clock. We had a good day out roaming around, playing, and throwing rocks. The teacher had an enjoyable day too with us being out of her hair.

After completing grades one through six at Bagwell, I transferred to Detroit Public School in Detroit, Texas. The new school was only about five miles from my home in Bagwell. The introduction to organized sports was new to me. Playing ball with classmates and friends was the extent of what I knew of sporting events. Watching sporting events on television was something I did not grow up doing. I was twelve years old before we got our first television. When I enrolled in athletics my seventh grade year, basketball was the main sport as football was not offered at the time. The coach teaching me how to dribble was challenged. After a few practices, I thought the coach was going to give up on me. My dribbling skills were not very good, and if you are short and cannot dribble, there is not much you can contribute to the team. I have often thought if my coach had given up on me, the future course of my life would have changed. My shooting skills, though, were my strength. When I started shooting set shots, the coach took notice. Shooting baskets in the dark at home had paid off. I guess if you can score consistently in darkness, one should have no problem in daylight.

After he saw me hit shot after shot in a set position, he devised a coaching strategy. When it was time for our first game, he told me, "Don't even try to dribble. Just go down and get to the wing area of the court and wait for your teammates to get you the ball. Then shoot it."

He did not have to tell me to shoot it because that was all I could do anyway. I set up on the wing area of the court about twenty feet from the basket. My teammates got me the ball, and my very first shot was nothing but net. The swoosh sound was the same whether in daylight or darkness.

After that first game, basketball became my obsession. I could not get enough. I wanted to learn how to dribble and continue to improve my overall skills. How was I to know as a seventh grade boy how basketball would play a role in my life as an adult? The mental toughness that began by completing chores and other assigned duties at home two miles north of town and playing basketball would help me face future life challenges.

The enjoyment of competing was much fun. My seventh through twelfth grade years passed quickly. Sports had become part of my life. In spring 1965, my high school coach informed me that Paris Junior College in Paris, Texas, had an interest in me to play basketball. They were prepared to offer me a scholarship if I wanted to continue my education. Needless to say, my dribbling skills had improved, and my set shot had given way to a jump shot. Even though basketball, the competition, the nature of the sport, as well as the spirit of the game were all greatly enjoyed, their offer was declined, and I thanked them for their interest in me as an athlete. The motivating factor behind my decision was my high school sweetheart. After graduation, I got a job with the Campbell Soup Company in Paris, Texas, and we decided to get married. It was a decision that I would live to regret. My parents tried to talk me out of my decision at this stage in my life, but it landed on deaf ears.

The marriage lasted about a year and half with no children born from this union. For this I am grateful. Talking and reconciling were not options. The divorce was granted, and we went our separate ways.

This was an unsettling time in my life. I left Campbell Soup and started to work at Red River Army Depot in Texarkana, Texas. The biggest mistake I had made at this point was not taking my parents' advice. Later, as I looked back on this time, I could better understand why my parents asked me not to marry so young. As I grew older, the answer was my parents became smarter.

In summer 1967, my brother and his wife invited me to live with them and go to college. They lived in Liberty, a small community just outside Conway, Arkansas. So I left Texas and crossed the Red River into Arkansas.

A quote from the great baseball pitcher Satchel Paige came to mind, "Don't look back. Something might be gaining on you." I didn't look back, and the next thing I saw was a sign that said "Land of Opportunity."

Crossing Red River and never looking back.
(Illustration by Myra Baugh)

Opportunity had evaded me thus far in life because of poor judgment and bad choices. I enrolled at the University of Central Arkansas in fall 1967, deciding that my major would be physical education because I wanted to be a coach. When I met with my advisor for the first time, he set up a four-year plan that guided me in that direction, along with a minor in social studies. For a freshman entering college, getting enrolled in classes, finding my classrooms, learning my professors' names, getting the required instructional materials for each of my classes, and finding the cafeteria were all necessary tasks for beginning the first day.

The fun part came next: locating where students gathered to just hang out or play cards between classes. It did not take long to fit in to that fun-filled place and make new friends. Learning the different card games was somewhat of a challenge, yet I was fully aware that all play could result in not achieving my goal of graduating and receiving my BSE degree. Therefore, I struck a balance between studies and fun. Looking back, though, hanging out with fellow classmates and playing cards was much more fun than being engaged in classroom studies.

After attending three full years, including summer terms, I was set to graduate in August 1970. In the spring, I started looking for coaching/teaching opportunities. There happened to be an opening in Magazine, Arkansas, for a coach. The only problem was they needed someone to start June 1 to coach and oversee the summer baseball program, but I still needed six college hours to complete my degree and graduate in August. I made an appointment with the principal of the school and informed him that I needed six hours to graduate. The baseball program was in the afternoon and at night, so I proposed to complete the three hours of credit in the morning both summer terms and work the baseball program during the afternoon and evening. He took my proposal under advisement and said he would get back to me. He called within two days to ask if I could come to the school for another interview. I accepted and met with him and the superintendent. They were agreeable to my proposal and offered me the job, which I accepted.

I thought back to when I crossed the Red River leaving Texas just three years earlier and saw the "Land of Opportunity" sign. My thoughts had been about moving toward a teaching/coaching profession that was then just a dream but was soon about to become a reality. This opportunity was all that I wanted, and I got it.

On Thursday, May 28, 1970, I signed my first teaching contract with Magazine Public School in Magazine, Arkansas. The effective starting date was on Monday, June 1. I started thinking about living quarters. The problem was I didn't have enough money to rent anything until my first payday, which was a month away. What to do? I explained my dilemma to the principal. I had only four days to get settled somewhere in town before starting work. The principal informed me that his mother had an extra room in her home since she lived by herself. After the principal talked it over with her, she said it would be all right.

This was more than I could have hoped for! Moving was not a problem. Wherever I went, everything I owned was always with me. I got settled in over the weekend and made plans to begin work on Monday. My baseball coaching duties were mainly making the field ready for play, planning the umpires' schedules, handling crowd control, and turning the field lights on and off.

The principal's mother made dinner for me most every night. I had to ask myself why everyone was being so nice. A few days before, I was unknown to them and the townspeople. Now I had a place to stay and nightly meals furnished, and I was waiting on my first paycheck. When my first paycheck arrived, I offered to pay for my room and board, but the principal's mother would not accept any money. This was one of those unexpected blessings in my life.

In August, just across the street from the school, a mobile home became available to rent and I took it. I thanked the principal and his mother for their hospitality and generosity, with special appreciation to his mother for all of those great meals she cooked.

By the first week in August, the summer baseball program was completed for the year. The summer went quickly. The three-hour British Lit II course was coming to an end. This was one tough course taken under the head of the English department. The poems, short stories, and literary works I studied were challenging. I just wanted to pass the course and move on with my life. Finals were on Thursday, August 13. Graduation was set for Friday, August 14 in the afternoon. I was anxious to know my final grade before walking across the stage. So on Friday morning I went to the professor's office and check the bulletin board just outside his office door to see if grades had been posted. They had not, but the professor happened to be in his office.

I knocked on his door and he invited me in, saying, "What can I do for you, Mr. Cogburn?"

I asked if he had my final grade for the course. He said no. I explained that I had already signed a teaching/coaching contract with Magazine School.

He said, "That's good, Mr. Cogburn."

I also said my contract would only be valid if I passed this course. The professor acknowledged my concern by saying, "Well, Mr. Cogburn, I hope you pass the course."

At that point, I knew that any further dialogue would not

be productive, so I looked toward the door to exit. I thanked him for his time and left.

Around 1:00, I decided to go back to the professor's office to check the bulletin board again to see if the grades were now posted, and they were! My grade was a C. I jumped for joy. I couldn't wait to walk across the stage to receive my bachelor of science in education diploma. Graduation was a personal goal I had set, and on August 14, 1970, I achieved it! My brother Buddy and his wife, Esther, who lived nearby, came to watch me graduate along with my mother, who had driven from Detroit, Texas, a distance of 240 miles to celebrate her baby son's achievement.

That afternoon, when I walked across the stage to receive my diploma, I looked at the professor.

He responded with a sly facial expression, a smirky grin, and a nod as if to say, "Congratulations." He knew the anxiety that I felt that morning when I came by his office and the suspense of not knowing whether I had passed the course.

The first day of the Magazine school year was

Tuesday, September 2. This was a big day for a first-year teacher learning the ropes, so to speak. We had teachers' meetings the previous week. Even with those meetings, the administrators only covered a few things. The rest was up to the individual teacher to learn for himself. My classroom teaching assignment was one class of seventh-grade history, an all-boy class. During one of our teacher training sessions, the principal gave us a warning that students would try and test us to see what we would tolerate and what they could get away with.

He informed us that we should, "Stay firm and be in charge of your classroom."

My educational courses, teacher training sessions, and all other discussions concerning human behavior would not prepare me to understand the mind of seventh-grade boys. My lesson plans were prepared, and with my grade book in hand, I entered the building on the first day of the school year, full of excitement at beginning my career as a teacher.

I introduced myself to the class and then wrote my name

on the chalkboard. Next, I wanted to get to know my students, so I passed a roll sheet around the room. Each student was to write his name on it. Then I handed out their textbooks so they could write their names and tell me the book numbers, which I recorded in my grade book. By the time this was finished, the class period had ended. I was, however, able to give a class assignment to read the first ten pages of chapter one in the text for discussion the next day.

My assessment of the class after only the first day had me wondering what the second day with twenty-two rambunctious, noisy, and wild boys would look like. I decided to go to the principal that evening and ask for his advice. I explained my first day's observation of my class.

After listening, he knew that my seventh-grade boys class could get out of control if left unchecked. His reply was, "Don't put up with any form of misbehavior during class." He also stated if I needed his assistance to let him know.

On the second day, I was in my room long before class started. I had my grade book with all of my students' names recorded and my lesson plans. The bell rang and the students entered and took their seats, and after welcoming them all, I started with roll call. I then asked everyone to open their textbooks to begin discussing the first ten pages that had been assigned for homework. I turned to write the highlights of those pages on the chalkboard when someone in the back of the room threw a large spit wad that stuck for a moment on the chalkboard just to the right of me.

When I turned, I caught a glimpse of someone in the back of the room being noticeably active. The class all laughed and had their moment of a good time. For me, this was one educational moment that was not covered in my college courses. This was purely an on-the-job training course made possible by seventh-grade boys. I immediately asked John Doe to step out into the hall to talk about this matter. I then asked if he was the one who threw the spit wad. He hesitated for a moment, but then said yes.

I said, "John, this is the second day of the school year, and

I'm taking up class time to deal with this spit wad incident, which should have never happened."

That's when I called for the principal and turned the matter over to him. I was beginning to see more clearly as a new teacher why this type of behavior was not covered in college courses or in-service training. The fact is, there are no psychology courses or any other courses that can predict the understanding or behavior of a seventh-grade boy.

Basketball was the reason I attended college, and I was looking forward to my coaching career. At Magazine, I was hired to coach the junior girls, junior boys, varsity girls, and varsity boys. The first day of practice consisted of scheduling physical exams with a doctor, assigning lockers, handing out practice uniforms and shoes, and getting to know the players and they got to know me as their coach.

The second day of practice consisted of shooting drills as well as defensive drills. Each of my teams' class periods went fast. There never seemed to be enough time during regular class periods to accomplish all the daily objectives. I never thought of coaching as being a job. It was more like a recreational activity I looked forward to every day. Each team had been working hard to achieve the goals they set. Basketball season was only about two weeks away, and I was still assessing individual players for the starting lineup.

Marilyn and Johnny

Sunday, October 4, 1970, was sunny, with temperatures between sixty and seventy degrees. I began the day by attending church at 10:00 in Booneville. After worship, I went to my favorite restaurant, the Booneville Bearcat, for lunch. I went home, took a short nap until around 2:30, and then went to the school gym.

It was my customary routine to open the gym on Sunday afternoons to give the kids additional time to improve their shooting skills and interact with me. Some of my players were already there waiting on me to open the gym. This is always encouraging to a coach to have players eager to practice and improve their skills.

I began shooting baskets with the kids when two unexpected guests arrived. I was near the free-throw area of the court at the time and recognized one as a former student when I was a student teacher at Danville High. The other woman was a stranger. My former student had mentioned having an older sister when I had her in class and had wanted me to meet her. After that, it was only a passing thought.

My long-awaited coaching career had now started. This was an exciting time for me. My main interest was getting my teams prepared for the first basketball game of the season. Today, however, my focal point changed from basketball to admiring this attractive stranger.

As I slowly walked toward them, basketball didn't seem that important even though I had a ball in my hand at the time. My former student had decided to bring her sister to Magazine, population fewer than five hundred, to meet the newly hired coach of the Magazine Rattlers. The stranger was introduced to me as Marilyn. During our brief conversation, she spoke of her profession as being an English teacher.

My thoughts began spinning through my head. Was this stranger standing before me on this basketball court the person of my dreams? At first I suspected we both had mutual interests, but then my thoughts changed after we briefly conversed. I had to ask myself: *What does an English teacher really have in common with a basketball coach?* There are just so many verbs and adverbs to identify and discuss. The only thing I could think of to advance the conversation that might be of interest to an English teacher would be the short stories and poems that I had studied in the British Literature II class, which I had tried hard to forget. Now I was thinking, *Which poem or short story do I know enough about to actually discuss and would be one she might have an interest in?*

My brain search led me to one poem that I could identify with, one I had devoted much time to studying: "Ode on a Grecian Urn" by John Keats. The author is standing in front of an urn observing the visual art imagery depicted on the urn. That was something I could relate to the moment Marilyn arrived. She was this live image of beauty, a picture of art herself. Unlike the images on the urn, however, she could walk out the door and leave me to my own silent interpretation.

My brain became dead to conversation. I was beginning to feel like that bird in Edgar Allen Poe's poem, "The Raven," who could only say one word: "Nevermore."

In a scene on the urn from the third stanza of Keats's poem, a piper is portrayed playing happy songs to the carved images of a boy and a girl who never embraced but whose love has become immortalized, free from time yet frozen in time. The piper wishes for their future life together to be happy, filled with joyfulness and contentment. The author believes their love is "far above" that of ordinary humans' love.

Could Marilyn be that girl and I be that boy whose physical and spiritual life journey together was about to begin? I kept these thoughts about the poem and Marilyn to myself to use perhaps at another time to stir the conversation if and when the occasion presented itself. Only about five minutes had passed thus far from the time I was introduced to Marilyn. While we were still searching for words to continue the conversation,

I noticed Marilyn as being somewhat shy and that she had a quiet, reserved personality along with a gentle disposition. It was like I had become frozen in silence searching for words to say.

She had become so intriguing to me! There was something about this woman that already attracted me. She willingly drove approximately twenty-five miles with her sister to meet me, and now we no longer had anything to talk about. The conversation, as they say, "dried up." It was as though neither of us could think of anything more to say.

I was about to join in the scrimmage when I asked Marilyn to *hold my watch*. When she said yes, my mind ran wild with questions. Did she even like basketball? Would she get tired of holding my watch while watching me play? Yet she placed it on her wrist and held it for the entire scrimmage! My thoughts were like a coin toss at the beginning of a football game: *What call should I make? Should I thank them for coming and leave it at that? Or should I be more personal and ask if she would like to go to dinner or take in a movie sometime?*

Our meeting could have been easily passed off as just meeting a new friend, with each of us looking ahead to our careers and going our separate ways. We both had decisions to make concerning each other. Prayers are answered in many different ways to serve purposes. Oftentimes, when prayers are offered by faith, the answer to those prayers may take years or even be answered in ways that are unexpected. When they are finally answered, our intelligence may get in the way of recognizing the answer.

I had to make a spur-of-the-moment decision. One might think I was making this decision more complex than it really was, and that may have been true; however, I had prayed for a wife and partner for two years while I was in college. Was I to dismiss this as a casual meeting without giving it a chance or go ahead and ask her out?

Marilyn and I exchanged phone numbers and said our goodbyes. The ball, as they say, was now in my court. The only question was, was a Higher Power working here? What guidance going forward would help me determine my future relationship with a woman who came unexpectedly to the gym at three o'clock in the afternoon? How was I to know at the time that this precious moment was the beginning of a relationship of love, marriage, careers, and family and would be remembered for a lifetime?

The first week we conversed over the phone just getting to know each other. The second week, on Saturday, Marilyn invited me to her parents' home, Jimmy and Ruth Patterson, for dinner. Marilyn and her mother cooked a wonderful dinner of fried chicken, mashed potatoes, gravy, pinto beans, and dessert. There is an old saying, "The way to a man's heart is through his stomach." That meal still stirs my taste buds to this day. Though her cooking impressed me, I noticed Marilyn had such a good family, and they all had strong spiritual values, so I continued to call her.

Marilyn and I talked on the phone and went on dates to the movies and out to eat over the next few weeks when it did not interfere with my coaching duties. Marilyn had graduated from Arkansas Tech University in spring 1970 and signed a contract to teach seventh through twelfth grade English, beginning in the fall at Havana Public School in Havana, Arkansas. This was the beginning of a thirty-year teaching career for her. We continued dating and talking about our likes and dislikes and everything else young adults talk about when getting to know each other.

I struggled to know if she was the right one for me. When I looked into those big brown eyes and the pleasantness of her personality, her sincerity, honesty, love of children, and above all else her spiritual commitment to God, I knew. It was those attributes that were similar to mine that were taught to me by my parents. Proverbs 31:10 says, "Who can find a virtuous woman?" I found one.

By the first week of December, after only two months of dating, I made my decision to ask Marilyn to marry me! I prayed she would say yes, and my prayers were answered!

On Thursday, December 31, 1970, at five o'clock, Marilyn and I were united in holy matrimony at the church in Morrilton, Arkansas. Charles Banes, a longtime friend and minister, performed the ceremony.

Though I had saved enough money to purchase a ring for Marilyn, I didn't have enough money to buy one for myself. When the minister asked for the ring, Marilyn had to pretend she was putting it on my finger. In writing from memory of our wedding day, a song sung by Don Williams comes to mind titled: "I am Just a Country Boy." The lines of the song that I relate are "money have I none," "never could afford a store-bought ring," and "all I could afford is a loving heart, the only one I own." Within about six months we had saved enough money to purchase a ring for me.

Marilyn was so beautiful! She was twenty-two and I was twenty-four. What a grand and happy time for both of us! We were not financially able to have an opulent wedding, but our small wedding attended by family and friends was simple and filled with love, and that was what really mattered. We had a two-day honeymoon in Conway, Arkansas, because we both had to be at work on Monday, but none of that mattered because we loved each other. This was the beginning of our journey together both personally and professionally.

January 3 was our first Sunday to worship together as husband and wife. Our spiritual walk together began with a prayer of thankfulness to God for bringing our lives together. After our prayer, we attended church at Booneville. Marilyn and I had already discussed the importance of praying, attending church, going to Bible classes at church, studying the Bible together, and meeting with others with similar Christian values to share and discuss how they coped with daily life struggles. These were all important characteristics for our spiritual growth.

After a few weeks attending church, Marilyn wanted to make a new commitment to Christ. She already had a strong faith and belief in Jesus Christ as being the son of God. Now she wanted to renew her faith by reenacting the death, burial, and resurrection of him in her life. Upon her confession that Jesus is the Christ, the Son of God, she was baptized for the forgiveness of sins and raised out of water a new disciple of Christ (see Romans 6:3–6 New International Version for more information).[1]

The second semester began on Monday, January 4. My basketball teams were playing in several tournaments and many regular season games. Marilyn was working hard to keep up with all the activities at her school as well as attending basketball games with me. During away games, she rode the bus with me and my team and sat on the bleachers just behind me to cheer. I can still hear those cheers as if they happened only yesterday. What a fan, friend, and wife!

Our first paycheck we received jointly from our employment was an exciting day. We went on our first grocery shopping trip together. We were like two unrestrained kids walking the aisles of the store and filling our cart with all the items we wanted.

When we got home, we unloaded several bags of groceries. Two items that I remember are a block of Cracker Barrel cheese and Ritz crackers. We decided to eat some of that expensive cheese, but we did not have a kitchen knife. I got out my pocketknife and sliced the cheese with it. What food can be simpler to eat to begin a forty-eight-year journey than cheese and crackers? Our simple lifestyle was by choice.

We only had a few basketball games left before the season was over. My, how time flies when you're having fun! Overall, we had won more games than we lost. I was proud of my players and how competitive they were along with the good sportsmanship they displayed whether they won or lost.

Now it was time to get ready for baseball season. It was still hard for me to believe that I was getting a salary to do something that was fun each and every day. As I reflect on my twenty-four-year coaching career, there were not many days that I was absent from school. Some days I should have been absent because of sickness, but I chose to go anyway.

In the second week in May 1971, we were playing the last game of the season with Scranton on their field, scheduled for a 2:00 start time. We had a good, competitive game. As I recall, we lost by a couple of runs. After it ended, good sportsmanship was shown by both teams. I, along with my managers, gathered the equipment to place on the bus to get started back home.

That's when a stranger who had been watching came out of the bleachers and headed across the baseball field toward me. I didn't know who he was, what to expect, or what he was going to say.

He began by saying, "Coach Cogburn, I'd like to have a word with you."

He introduced himself as the superintendent of Van Cove schools, a small, rural school located between Mena and DeQueen, Arkansas, on Highway 71 about eighty miles south.

He said, "I know you want to get started home, so I'll make this brief. I need a basketball coach, a principal, and an English teacher for the high school beginning next school year."

While he spoke, I thought, *I already have a job.* I had just gotten married and was settled in Magazine. Everyone had been so nice and helpful to Marilyn and me. These thoughts spun around in my head.

He continued. "I know your wife is a good English teacher. I'm prepared to offer you and your wife a contract with the district."

I replied, "I'm not qualified to be a principal."

He replied, "Your title to the state Department of Education will be assistant to the superintendent, but your title at school will be principal and coach."

When I moved to Magazine less than a year before, I was still in college, traveling to Conway each day both summer terms. The last term, I spent the first half of the day in the English department studying short stories, poetry, and British literary works. Then I would travel back to Magazine the second half of the day to get the baseball field ready for play at night. All during that summer semester, I was wondering if I would even pass the courses to continue my employment with the school district. I didn't have a wife. I was homeless. I had no money for housing and was waiting on my first paycheck.

Magazine had been good to me, and as I thought back over this first year, the Van Cove superintendent continued, "I am prepared to offer you a $7,800 yearly contract to be my principal and coach along with an additional $1,200 to oversee the student work program during the summer. The district will also pay your electricity to live in a mobile home on campus. Your wife will be offered a $6,300 contract to teach English."

Wow! This guy just came out of the bleachers and walked across the baseball diamond to fill my head with dollar signs. The contracts he was offering Marilyn and me were more money than we had seen thus far in our lifetime! This was another unexpected moment.

I informed him we needed a couple of days to think about it, talk it over, and then give him a call.

Marilyn and I had very little in monetary assets. We both worked our way through college thanks to national defense student loans, and we were under a program that after five years of teaching and making loan payments, half the loan would be forgiven. We both knew the value of hard work to achieve individual, financial, family, and spiritual goals.

It didn't take us long to add up the benefits in the offer made by the superintendent. We would receive a nice salary increase. Our employment would be at the same school. The mobile home we would have to purchase would be located on the school campus, plus the electricity would be paid for by the district, and we could walk to our jobs.

Before making our final decision, we wanted to visit the school and to get a feel of the town. So I called the superintendent to set up a time to come for a visit. Marilyn and I were only available on the weekend, so we scheduled our appointment for Saturday, May 22, 1971.

We left Magazine around 8:30 and arrived at Cove between 10:30 and 11:00. We drove to his home, which was located across the street from the school. He and his wife had lunch prepared for us. After a good visit and a great homecooked meal, he and his wife took us on a tour of the school. His wife was also a teacher. She showed Marilyn her classroom where she would spend most of the school day. The superintendent showed me my office, which was located across the hall from his. Then we all went on a tour of the gym where much of my time would be spent.

After completing the tour and all questions were answered, we made our decision to accept his offer. My contract would become effective July 1. Marilyn's would be effective when school started in August. We would have more than a month to purchase a mobile home, get it moved on campus, and then move from Magazine.

The transition went well, and we found a used mobile home that had been well maintained and fit our budget of $3,800. We hired an individual to move the home and get it all set up by the middle of June. We moved everything we owned in our two vehicles from our rented mobile home in Magazine to our new home in Cove. The home was furnished with a stove, refrigerator, a nice couch, chair, and a dinette table with four chairs. The only furnishings we needed to purchase were a bed, mattress, box spring, TV, and antenna. We got moved, settled, and had a few days to relax and shop for things we previously couldn't afford.

The superintendent's wife had a huge aquarium that was fascinating to watch, with all the rocks, miniature caves, and plastic see-through tunnels. She had it stocked with guppies. The noise of rustling water was so relaxing. She informed us that, after a long day working with kids, to come home and just sit and watch the fish and listen to the water was so therapeutic. Marilyn and I decided to get an aquarium. We did some research as to what type of fish would be compatible and decided guppies would be best suited. The superintendent's wife gave us several to begin stocking our own aquarium.

I began work on July 1 and got acquainted with the six students who were on the school work program, of which I would be in charge. We began painting, cleaning, mopping floors, and making classrooms ready for the new school year. On Friday, July 16 I received a phone call from my brother Benny. Our father was very ill and had been taken to the hospital and placed in ICU in Paris, Texas.

Marilyn and I packed overnight bags and left Cove on Saturday morning to see him. He was resting comfortably. We spent the night with my brother and his wife. On Sunday afternoon, I went to see my father for the last time before leaving for Cove to get ready to start work Monday morning.

I can still hear his final words to me: "I love you, son."

I replied, "I love you, Dad." Those last words spoken between a father, mother, son, or daughter, whichever the case may be, are words that never grow old and are remembered for a lifetime.

On many weekends we traveled to Danville to visit Marilyn's parents. Marilyn would take her mother shopping and out to eat at her favorite restaurant, Old South in Russellville. The diner opened its doors in 1947, and its appearance has not changed much in the years since. Marilyn's father, Jimmy, took me fishing or hunting depending on the time of year or season. I suppose Lake Ouachita was his all-time favorite lake for fishing; however, any lake, river, or stream would be his preference if fish were biting.

On one of those trips in the late summer of 1972, Marilyn's brothers, uncle, two cousins, a family friend, her dad, and I left Danville before daylight and headed to Lake Ouachita. We launched our boats and searched for schooling bass. This is a search and wait process. When one surfaces, you cast your artificial lure in hopes that the fish will mistake your bait for shade.

This happened to be one of those trips that only come once

in a lifetime. After we launched our boats, we were still early on the lake, and fish typically school later in the morning. The weather, wind, and many other factors play a part in having a good fishing day. We were all sitting around in our boats trying to keep cool, drinking plenty of water and enjoying the mountain terrain. Between nine and ten o'clock, the sky became overcast, which was somewhat welcome on that one hundred-degree morning.

All of a sudden there seemed to be an explosion of fish surfacing in the narrow cove of the lake. They were rolling on top of the water; it was such a sight to behold! Never had I seen this many fish in such a small area. The school was the circumference of a small house, and the cove was narrow, so we had to dock our boats. Then we got out on the bank to cast our lures. We caught fish one after another, as fast as we could take one off our hook, place it behind us on the bank, and cast again. The action was fast for about fifteen to twenty minutes. The fish ranged from two to three pounds each. There were eight of us, and we all caught our limit. It was a day of fishing that I will remember forever!

Teaching and Coaching Years

Marilyn was happy to partner with me on the coaching circuit. My lovely wife was eager to keep the charts or books, whichever was needed. I played in the championship game at Dierks Invitational Tournament against Lockesburg. We had already played them in home and away games. Though the games were hard fought and scored in the eighties, we lost both by three points: one game by one point and the other by two.

My players grew weary of me reminding them of the outcomes in both games, yet they assured me this upcoming game three would be different! My coaching strategy changed as well from a high-scoring game to a low-scoring game, with emphasis on defense and ball control. The game plan was simply each time we had possession of the ball, one to two minutes of time were to be run off the clock before taking a close-in shot, preferably a layup. In the previous two games, Lockesburg had double- and sometimes triple-teamed my outstanding six foot, four inch player. Our defense, for the first half of play, would be a one-three-one zone.

Upon arrival at the gym, Marilyn went straight to the scoring table and sat next to the official bookkeeper, whose book decides the game winner. Marilyn recorded the opposing team's lineup in our books and then gave me the names and numbers of their starting five.

It was now game-time tipoff. My players were disciplined and talented and followed the game plan perfectly. We kept control of the ball, so the game was controlled by us as well. By the end of the first eight minute quarter, we held the lead eight to six. As the half came to an end, our lead was extended sixteen to twelve! The game was most intense because we were holding the ball, running time off the clock, and taking shots close to the basket.

It was now time for the second half tipoff. The game was heating up with much intense play. I changed the defense to a full-court man-to-man. Our opponent had become anxious and frustrated because we were controlling the game and taking selective shots. By the end of the third quarter, the score was tied at twenty-four. Because of the way we played the previous three quarters, the fourth quarter began with some of their key players in foul trouble.

In the last minute of the game, my six feet, four inch post drew a two-shot foul. He stepped to the free-throw line to shoot. The first shot missed but the second scored. That's when Marilyn, being vigilant, watched the official scorekeeper incorrectly give the point to Lockesburg. She immediately informed me. I called a timeout to confer with the referees. The point was correctly changed and awarded to us. When the game was over and the official books were tallied, we won the game by a score of thirty-one to thirty. Thanks to Marilyn, the Van Cove Hornets won the championship trophy!

In 1974 we left Van Cove schools to accept a teaching/coaching position with the Bismarck School District located twenty miles south of Hot Springs on Highway 7. We had a good working relationship with the superintendent, school board, and community while at Cove; however, my duties as a principal, along with my coaching responsibilities were mentally exhausting. So we sold our mobile home and moved into a furnished house provided for the coach and his family at Bismarck. We got an increase in salary as well.

In April, Lake DeGray State Park, located about two miles from our home in Bismarck, opened. We had heard the fishing was great, so we decided to purchase a small flat-bottomed boat. Marilyn and I would often go out to fish or just sail around to observe the beauty of the lake. Marilyn never fished much. She watched me catch my limit of bass, which we would take home, fillet, and eat along with french fries, coleslaw, and hush puppies. Talk about good!

We spent many recreational hours on the lake fishing, having picnics, and enjoying being together. In September, not long after school had started, I contracted the mumps. I was unable to do anything for two weeks except keep my feet propped up higher than my head. Marilyn would come home every day during her noon conference break to prepare lunch and assist me with my needs. What a partner!

The school year went fast. After one year at Bismarck, we both wanted to move closer to Marilyn's family and friends in Danville. We checked for teaching and coaching openings. Our search for schools that needed an English teacher and a coach led us to Ola, Arkansas, a small rural town located in Yell County about eleven miles east of Danville. Ola had a population of about five hundred at the time. Marilyn signed a contract to teach seventh- to twelfth-grade English, and I signed a contract as head basketball coach, assistant football coach, and Jr. girls and varsity girls track coach.

Marilyn was pregnant with the first of our three daughters. We found two acres of land for sale two miles west of Ola on Highway 10. We purchased the land and bought a new mobile home. The house was set up, and we moved in the week of June 1, 1974.

In the early morning hours of June 6, I took Marilyn to the hospital in Danville. About midmorning, Marilyn gave birth to our first daughter, who we named Shelly Elizabeth. Having our first child was the beginning of learning how to be a parent. The task was not easy. There were the diapers, the bottles, the baby bed (which we had already set up), the rocking chair, which was vital for the care of a newborn, and the waking up during the night for feeding. Shelly was up most of the night and slept most of the day. Marilyn and I shared night duty, which consisted of feeding, rocking, placing a pacifier in her mouth, and more rocking. I believe we wore out one rocking chair on our first daughter, and the second daughter hadn't arrived yet. There's an old saying, "You pay for your raising." If that saying is true, my parents had much difficulty in raising me.

More than a year had passed. We discovered a house for sale located across the street from the school. We decided to try to get a home loan from the bank. Attached was an extra lot that was included in the purchase price, a good investment for a young family. We bought the house, sold our mobile home on the two acres of land, and made a small profit. We moved into our home across the street from the school.

Marilyn was pregnant with our second daughter. She was born on November 14, 1975. We named her Leslie Kay. Shelly, our firstborn, was now two years old. We had finally gotten her to sleep better at night. We found a babysitter not far from our home. Marilyn prepared both our daughters for the daily trip to the sitter's house. Then she would get to school by 7:45 to begin preparing for the school day. I don't know how she kept up with all the responsibilities of her job, raising a growing family, keeping the house clean, and cooking our meals. I helped her with many of these chores, but she felt most comfortable doing them herself. The so-called baby boomer generation was made up of women, such as Marilyn, who worked hard all their lives to provide their children with an opportunity to achieve a quality of life through education. I can only say this: history will testify to and applaud the work ethic, commitment, and toughness of a special group of people born to that generation.

In spring 1978 we came up with a plan to build a new home on that extra lot we had purchased. Then we sold the home we were living in. We talked to the banker about our plans, and with the amount of equity we already had in the house, the banker was willing to subdivide the property and give us the loan to build a new house on that extra lot. We hired a contractor to start building our home, which was completed by fall 1978. The dream of owning a new home that Marilyn and I had worked and planned for had now come true.

The times she enjoyed with our young family in our new home were most memorable. Shelly was three and Leslie was one. The first Christmas we helped our daughters write letters to Santa and list the toys they wanted him to bring. Two toys I remember the most were a doll house and a miniature stove that had cabinets above the stovetop.

After we got our daughters to bed on Christmas Eve, Marilyn and I assembled the dollhouse and stove with screwdrivers and other tools. I estimated the time to complete the project would be about two hours. Boy was I wrong! Two hours had passed, and we only had a few pieces assembled and were still looking at the instructions. Marilyn was overseeing the project and holding parts for me to bolt together. After two a.m. I panicked somewhat because our daughters would be getting up early and seeing "Santa" assembling a toy that should have been assembled at the North Pole. The parts were scattered all over the floor. Three a.m. arrived and the instructions on how to assemble were giving me fits! I had a few more pieces assembled, but I was still a long way from having it completed. After much stress, we finally completed the project at four in the morning! The surprised looks on our daughters' faces were well worth the time and effort. Merry Christmas to our daughters with love from Santa, Mom, and Dad.

Marilyn and I had been married eight years. These were years of adjusting to married life as well as becoming parents. We had so much fun with our daughters Shelly and Leslie, taking them to church, reading Bible stories to them, sitting on the floor playing dolls, and taking them to Petit Jean State Park to swim and have picnics. I built a sandbox under the deck of our new house. They spent much time playing with their toys in the sand. Marilyn spent much of her time bathing and washing the sand from their hair. We must not forget all those trips to McDonald's in Russellville for those Happy Meals to get the toy that was included in the meal. We made trips to Marilyn's parents' house to celebrate Christmas and other holidays. Marilyn's lifelong friends would have gatherings at their houses to celebrate birthdays, holidays, events, or any occasion they could think of to get together and visit.

The five years we spent with the Ola School District were good years. I had good athletes and good teams. The Class A Girls State Track Championship was won in 1978 by some outstanding athletes who were also excellent academic students.

Ola Girls' track team Class A State Champion, 1978 (From left to right, top row: Kathryn Nail, Susan Pitts, Coach Johnny Cogburn, Debbie Otto, Paula Wood, Vicky Porter; Bottom row from left to righ: Darla Burnett, Debbie George, Susan Chancellor, Becky Buford, and Lisa Robinson.)

Many of the athletes that I coached while at Ola still contact me to reminisce about those sporting events and games of long ago. Marilyn and I made many friends at school and in the community. Unfortunately, the possibility of change can be expected as a coach, which I accepted when I chose to enter the profession. The school year of 1980 to '81, I signed a contract with the Havana School District to teach high school history.

I commuted a distance of about twenty-five miles from Ola. Marilyn continued teaching at the Ola school.

The following year there was an opening in Danville for a high school English teacher. Marilyn applied and was hired. She signed a contract for the 1981–82 school year. We decided to sell our home in Ola and move to Danville. At the time, the Danville Motel needed a manager. I applied for the position and was hired. The facility also had living quarters for the resident manager. We completed the sale of our home in Ola in July and moved into those living quarters with our two daughters. Shelly was now seven and Leslie five. Marilyn was pregnant with our third daughter.

Instead of hiring help to service the motel, Marilyn and I cleaned the rooms, changed the bedding, washed the sheets and linens, cleaned the toilets, and mopped the floors. These were all familiar duties to us. Marilyn and I worked these jobs while going to college, so our experience paid off. Also, we were rather tight with our expenditures. I guess that is why we got along so well. Money was never a problem in our marriage because we were not accustomed to having any before we got married. When we got married, we began on equal footing. Now that we were able to acquire a few extra dollars, we didn't want to give them away to someone else to do a job we both had plenty of experience doing.

Marilyn and I worked in the motel until it was time for her to report to school for in-service training the last week in August. I then took over the cleaning duties. School had just gotten started and was in session for about a week when I loaded Marilyn into our station wagon and traveled to St. Mary's Hospital in Russellville, where she gave birth to our third daughter, whom we named Rachel Lynn. She was born on Tuesday, September 8, 1981, at 9:50 a.m. Marilyn and our baby daughter were dismissed from the hospital on Wednesday, September 9. We had three daughters, so the two-bedroom motel suite where we were living had gotten smaller the day I brought Rachel and her mother home from the hospital.

We continued to work in the motel until the spring. Then we found an older house to purchase. It was one that we both liked, though it needed some remodeling to make it suitable for our young family. The remodeling project was completed by fall. Then we moved from the motel into our newly remodeled home.

I left my motel management position to open a barbecue restaurant and recreation center in Danville. I briefly left the coaching profession to explore the possibilities of becoming a business owner. Marilyn continued her employment with the Danville schools. Our daughter Shelly was now in first grade, and Leslie and Rachel were taken daily to the babysitter, who was one of Marilyn's lifelong friends.

After more than a year in the restaurant business, I decided to get back into the coaching profession. The amount of time spent working and running the business and the monetary reward for my time was not worth it.

In the summer, there was a coaching opening at Central Arkansas Christian (CAC) in North Little Rock for a junior high football coach and basketball coach, so I decided to apply for the position. I was hired for the 1983–84 school year.

I was now back into a more familiar profession. I bought a travel trailer, stayed during the weekdays, and came home on weekends. By the end of my school term with CAC, Marilyn and I looked into the possibilities of exploring teaching and coaching opportunities near my family in Texas.

So far Marilyn had thirteen years of experience and I had eleven. At the time, Texas teachers' salaries were considerably higher than salaries paid to teachers in Arkansas. This was our main reason for wanting to move. Another reason was to be closer to my family. So during the summer of 1984, Marilyn and I packed our station wagon and pickup truck fitted with plywood sideboards, loaded our three daughters, and started our five-hour journey to Sulphur Springs, Texas. We stayed one night in a motel. The next day we rented an apartment, and on day three, we began our search for placement in our teaching fields.

I found a coaching opening with the North Hopkins School District located about ten miles west of Sulphur Springs. Marilyn found an opening to teach English with the Greenville

School District located about twenty-five miles southwest of town. We applied for the positions and were hired. Marilyn signed her contract for $19,300. My contract was set at $21,500. This was a great day for us and our kids. Our salaries had almost doubled from the previous school year.

With our employment secured, we had the monumental task of raising our young family, Shelly (age ten), Leslie (eight), and Rachel (two) in a new town where we knew no one. We had to secure childcare for Rachel, so we asked friends from church for recommendations. After much searching, we settled on Lolly Pop Kids Stop, which was a mom-and-pop daycare facility. We got involved in the community through school activities and church. Of course, with a young family we spent a vast amount of time getting our kids to and from school and all their extracurricular activities. Watching them perform was great fun.

After a year and a half, Sulphur Springs had an opening for an eighth-grade English teacher. This was closer to our home than the Greenville position, so Marilyn applied and was hired.

Greenville found a replacement. Marilyn was released from that contract and began her fourteen-year career at Sulphur Springs. Our daughters were educated there as we continued living the American dream.

Birthday celebrations were always fun. Marilyn either prepared a homecooked meal, or we went out to eat at a local restaurant. Afterward, we would come home to enjoy the cake she had baked, followed by singing "Happy Birthday." What a blessed wife, mother, and friend!

As teachers, the holidays were always welcomed; welcomed for the time off from school to rest, relax, and recharge as well as to celebrate the occasion with our families and friends. During the Christmas season, a day trip to the Galleria in Dallas was always on our calendar. To watch our kids and my sister's kids ice skate was fun! Then we went shopping for that special gift for that special person. After shopping, we ate at our favorite barbecue, Italian, or Mexican restaurant.

Christmas Eve was most memorable opening family gifts. We would each open a gift one at a time to savor the moment.

After the kids went to bed, Santa left surprise gifts under the tree to be opened Christmas morning. After opening Santa's gifts, we traveled to my mother's house to join other family members for great food and fellowship. A gala time was always enjoyed by all and remembered to this day in family circles.

After celebrating with my mother and family, we had enough time during Christmas break to visit Marilyn's family in Danville, where we celebrated Christmas a second time. The celebration was over good food and catching up on past events in Danville.

After celebrating with Marilyn's family, we then celebrated Christmas a third time with Marilyn's lifelong friends, the Fab Five, as they called themselves. The fellowship and trust that these five women cultivated over the years is unmatched. To have those memories with Marilyn is a blessing that will be cherished always. I believe I can speak on behalf of their husbands and say to witness and be part of their friendships was an honor!

Our dream life was now in its middle stage. At this point,

Marilyn and I were in our early forties, still vibrant and full of energy. We enjoyed going on vacations with my sister Mary, her husband, their four children, and my mother, Olevia. On one trip we all loaded up into two vehicles and traveled to Ouray, Colorado. We enjoyed swimming, camping, and cooking on an open fire, and we still talk about it at family gatherings. Another outing was a daytrip with them to the zoo in Dallas! What a day spent with family and the monkeys!

When our kids were young, Marilyn and her mother, Ruth, took them to Disney World in Orlando, Florida. In other trips we traveled to San Antonio, visited the Alamo, and ate lunch on the Riverwalk. Going to the beach in Galveston and swimming and touring the aquarium was fun!

Another time we went to Destin, Florida, to visit Marilyn's sister and her husband. We also went to Hot Springs, Arkansas, and stayed at the historic Majestic Hotel. Then there were the trips to Branson, Missouri. The musical shows were enjoyed with family and friends. I recall the time spent at Silver Dollar City watching our kids and my sister's kids participating in a frog-racing contest. The contest was entertaining, full of laughter, and much fun. In thought, I relive the time Marilyn and I spent at the dinner theater aboard the Branson Belle, a romantic evening long remembered enjoying each other's company. These are only a few of the many vacations we took as a family, and we are blessed to have those memories.

During the school year, we spent quality time with our kids playing tennis at the local city park. Marilyn enjoyed playing tennis and was quite good. She and I would compete in singles, and more often than not she outperformed me. It did not hurt my ego much because it was all in good fun. What a good companion!

After the tennis workouts, we went to the local fast food joint and had hamburgers and ice cream. Just watching our kids interact with their mother, whether playing tennis, being at home, or at the local restaurant brought so much pleasure to me as a husband and father. Marilyn offered our children so much support, encouragement, and guidance. This is a woman, mother, wife, and friend who became irreplaceable in my life.

When I was sad, she made my day brighter by just being near. When I was lonely and away from home, she kissed away the time over the phone. When I was broken-hearted, she mended it with her love. She offered me a tomorrow filled with joy and love. She gave so much and asked for so little in return. My love for her grew beyond measure.

When Marilyn and I would get home from work, we took quiet walks around the block after dinner to wind down after a long day. We talked about our day, and on many occasions retirement would come up. When would we retire? Where would we retire? I thought the future would be better than the present. My thoughts were misguided. The future may not follow a predictable path.

Many of the old western classic movies portray the bad guy ending up in Boot Hill and the good guy riding off into the sunset with a beautiful woman by his side to live happily ever after. God's plan may not always be the plan we envision for ourselves, but in reality, the future is not ours to predict.

As the years passed, our children grew up and achieved so many different awards and honors throughout their education. Shelly was involved in school and community plays. We enjoyed watching her perform. Rachel was involved in volleyball and softball. Our middle daughter, Leslie, was on the drill team and selected Hopkins County Dairy Queen. All three children graduated from college. Marilyn and I attended each graduation with a sense of pride in all their achievements.

Early retirement was only three years away. That said, there was one more coaching assignment ahead. In summer 1997, in the coaching association bulletin, I saw an ad for a coach in south Texas. Why did I pick up the phone to make the call? Because the salary was considerable, the phone call cheap, and my intentions were low to accept such a position in a small Class A school. The school in Moulton, Texas, was five hours driving time from Sulphur Springs where we were living. The school needed an assistant basketball, head cross-country, and golf coach. The call was made, and the principal was cordial in discussing the needs of the position being filled. Toward the end of the conversation, he offered me the position if I would come for an official interview.

My response was, "I need to talk it over with my wife and will call you later today."

He said, "Okay!"

After talking the offer over with Marilyn, whose cheers of support and encouragement were always present, and considering the separation that would follow for a period of time, we felt the increase in salary to boost my pension in retirement was worth the sacrifice. Marilyn was willing to step up as head of household and allow me to complete my career and retire early.

I called the principal back Wednesday afternoon and then booked an early morning flight for Thursday out of Love Field in Dallas. I arrived at Hobby International Airport in Houston, rented a car, and drove about an hour to make my 10:00 a.m. appointment. After meeting the principal, he gave me an abbreviated tour of the school because my time was limited to catch my return flight back home that evening. My assigned duties were discussed and gone over in detail. He then asked if I had any questions.

My reply was, "When is lunch?"

Besides, a coach only needs athletes, a whistle, a clipboard, and chalk for drawing plays on the gym floor. I thought that any questions that came to mind could be discussed over lunch.

Evidently, he thought the question was important and said, "Let's go! Lunch is on me."

That was what sealed the deal. After lunch, we went back to his office. My contract was already filled out and only needed my signature. I signed the contract, rented an apartment, returned to the airport, turned in my rental car, caught my flight to Dallas, and was back home in Sulphur Springs by 6:00 p.m. What a day!

The first part of August, Marilyn and I loaded up a bed, box spring, mattress, and some personal belongings and headed to my temporary home in Moulton. The cross-country season was only a few weeks away, and I had to begin preparing my junior girls, junior boys, varsity girls, and varsity boys teams for competition beginning the first week of September. They were all good athletes who worked hard, competed well, and won many meets. The girls team competed for the state title in Austin and finished in the top ten, along with one boy who competed individually and placed fifth in the state meet. I was pleased with my athletes and how well they performed.

Congratulations from George W. Bush, then Governor of Texas (Photo from Cogburn family album)

In basketball, the boys won back-to-back state titles in 1998 and 1999. President George W. Bush, then governor of Texas, awarded the championship medals to players and coaches on the University of Texas basketball court. To be part of such a program before retiring was an honor. Within two years, the athletes had competed on the state level in three sports: cross country, basketball, and golf. Marilyn and I were beginning to feel that Austin had become our third home! My stay as a coach with athletes in Austin competing in state competition was more than twenty-four days in two years.

The principal gave me the school credit card and said, "Compete well and have a good time."

This we were able to do. Our stay was in the best motels Austin had to offer. The teams picked their meals not at McDonald's but at the Longhorn Steakhouse, Red Lobster, and many other favorite places. What a way to close a twenty-four-year coaching career that started when Marilyn and I first met in the Magazine (Rattlers) gym in Arkansas and finished with Marilyn by my side in the Texas Longhorn gym in Austin! This journey could have only been imagined, dreamed, or written in fiction, yet it was lived and part of our life story.

Retirement and "the Retirement House"

During spring break 1998, Marilyn and I had already decided to retire in Arkansas, so she could live closer to her family. When school was out, we loaded up and began what some would call a working vacation. We stayed at Marilyn's mother's house in Danville and began a property search. We looked at several different places to build, but none were available at the time. So we started searching for property near Marilyn's sister and her husband, who lived on Hillside Drive in Dardanelle. We found property owned by a local businessman that was adjacent to Marilyn's sister and husband's property. Though the property was not for sale, we decided to contact the owner and ask if he would consider selling us two acres off his forty. He decided he would at a cost of $6,500 an acre. This price was agreeable to us. Now Marilyn and her sister would be neighbors.

The property was covered with a heavy growth of brush and timber so thick you could hardly walk through. Deer had made winding trails through the property, and a brook with flowing water enhanced by the freshly fallen snow was captured in an image taken not long after we purchased the property.

First picture of the undeveloped land for our home. (Photo taken by Johnny Cogburn)

Our retirement plans were beginning to take shape. Retiring early was a goal we had set. Now that property had been purchased, we could work the plan. In summer 1998, I was driving down Jefferson Street in Sulphur Springs and saw the city revenue office building being torn down. I decided to inquire about the lumber. The contractor in charge of tearing down the six thousand square foot building said the lumber would be sold to the public as recycled materials. We agreed upon a price, and I began hauling pickup load after pickup load of two by six, two by eight, and two by twelve boards and twenty-seven hundred square feet of tongue and groove pine flooring. It was all stacked neatly under tarps in our backyard. This type of vintage pine lumber is such a rare find. One of the boards was marked June 1927. When I saw the opportunity, I could not pass it up. I was never disappointed.

In summer 1999, Marilyn's brother, Danny, and I began building a fence on two sides of the two acres using crossties from Bagwell as posts. When I was a young boy, I played on the railroad tracks these ties came from. Spikes from some of these ties date back to 1946, the year I was born.

After we completed building the fence, we cleared the two acres. We worked for about a week, and at that point I realized the task was too great for just the two of us with a chain saw, an axe, and a rake. By this time summer was almost over, so I decided to hire a man who owned a bulldozer to finish clearing the land. When he finished, a huge brush pile needed to be burned. I asked the man to burn the pile when the weather was more favorable.

Spring 2000 was a hectic time of year for us. Rachel was graduating from high school and would be attending the University of Arkansas in the fall. I was anxious to complete leveling the ground and filling in holes where stumps of trees were removed. I bought a U-Haul truck from my brother for the purpose of transporting the lumber to Arkansas. In the early summer I began the task of hauling all six stacks of lumber from our backyard in Texas to the site of our future home in Arkansas. The job was not easy and took four trips to complete. When all the material was at the building site, I marveled at the stacks of lumber waiting before me. It was hard to believe Marilyn's future home was in those stacks of lumber all covered with tarp and ready for the carpenter's creation.

That summer was very hot, and my clothes were soaked with sweat each day. The hard work of making the ground ready for building was completed. My retirement was set for December 31, 2000. My coaching career had given way to a new chapter of my life, one that I was anxious to begin. I traded my coaching cap for a carpenter's cap.

In April 2001 we got our loan to fund our home. This was a milestone in our lives. I hired a backhoe operator to dig the pier and beam footing. Then the concrete for the footing was poured. After that, the underground utilities, rough-in plumbing, and concrete blocks were laid. Next, the rock fireplace was started. After three months, all the necessary things were in place to begin the construction phase of our home. I knew I would not be able to build the house without help, so I called a longtime friend and asked if he wanted to help me in the construction of our home. He agreed, "As long as it did not interfere with deer season," which was an understandable response.

The walk to the lumber yard was only a few feet from our house, and the walk was rewarding because those hauled materials were already paid for. We began putting down the two by six floor joists and then the tongue and groove pine flooring. This was the first phase of the construction. I guess everyone remembers where they were on September 11, 2001; my friend and I were near the fireplace area of the house putting down the flooring. Marilyn's nephew informed us of the tragedy.

I hired a crew to finish the framing, put on the roof, hang the vinyl siding, and put in the windows. This was all completed by Thanksgiving. Now we were ready for sheetrock and painting. This phase was completed in January 2002. The beauty of our home was taking shape.

Marilyn's retirement was set for January 1, 2002. We were in Arkansas celebrating Christmas and our anniversary. The church in Sulphur Springs held a going-away party for us on Wednesday, January 23. Then the next day, the school hosted a retirement party for Marilyn. She received a nice service plaque with many other personal gifts from friends. What a way to end a thirty-year career in education!

We had already moved most of our home furnishings to a storage facility in Dardanelle. That Friday, early in the morning, Marilyn and I said our goodbyes, packed up our belongings, and began our journey to Arkansas.

I had been staying with Marilyn's mother and brother throughout the building of our house. Now Marilyn and I would be together, at her mother's, until our house was ready.

We moved into our new home on Thursday, March 14, 2002. Even though the house was not fully completed, we were able to move in to part of it. A lifelong dream of drafting house plans, building the house, and then moving in was being realized.

Marilyn had retired, and two months later she moved

into her dream home. She was so happy to retire in a home that was built for her, and I was blessed to have built it for my wife, whose love for me was unwavering. It was this steadfast love that had sustained me all those years, and now I was able to give back to the woman who I'd prayed for before I knew her.

As we looked around our new home, we could hardly believe the beauty surrounding us. We were like two kids in a make-believe world. The afternoon we moved in was cold. As daylight gave way to night, I built a fire in our rock fireplace. The wood crackled as it burned. The warmth of the fire and the coziness of the living room made the sharing of each other's company most enjoyable.

The warmth and coziness of the fireplace.

(Photo taken by Johnny Cogburn)

The following day I completed sealing the floors and finished the trim. Now we were ready to furnish the living room, dining room, and remaining bedroom. Marilyn had such an enjoyable time shopping and choosing the right lamps, table, chairs, and couch as well as decorating with that warm, tender, personal touch.

The sunroom and the dining room/living room.

(Photos taken by Johnny Cogburn)

The fulfillment we felt after planning of our dream home had finally come true. We woke up early every morning to the brightness of the sun shining through our bedroom window. The birds chirped in the trees, as if to say, "It's time to get up." Each day, the freshness of the morning brought a renewed admiration of the beauty of the pine floors and the exposed wood throughout our home. We felt as though we were starting our lives over. Retiring in our fifties was a decision we made even though it meant giving up future income. That decision turned out to be a fourteen-year blessing. As we walked out of our kitchen with a cup of hot chocolate and coffee in hand headed to our porch swing, we observed the beauty of nature and felt a completeness in our lives together. Now the task of landscaping with crepe myrtles, roses, and shrubs would add to the beauty of the wraparound porch. The hanging baskets of flowers Marilyn placed uniformly around the porch added colorful beauty.

Marilyn's plants on the porch.
(Photo taken by Johnny Cogburn)

March 31, 2002, Easter Sunday, was a special day for us. As we sat on our porch swing and watched the sunrise, my thoughts turned toward spirituality. This was the day we celebrated the resurrection of our Lord and Savior, Jesus Christ. We began the day by attending worship services as was our custom every Sunday. As we worshiped and remembered what Jesus did for us on Calvary that day, we included prayers of thankfulness and blessing in our lives as always.

In April, as we sat on our porch swing, the fragrance of

petunias and honeysuckle filled the air. The dogwoods were in full bloom a short distance away. Birds were singing as nature surrounded our home with all its beauty! This was the created beauty that God allowed us to enjoy!

We began Mother's Day by watching the sunrise from the comfort of our porch while sipping cups of coffee and hot chocolate. We then went to church. Afterward, we went to lunch and I presented Marilyn with a dozen red roses. Roses were my mother's choice of flowers. Mother's Day is special to us as we reflect on the wonderful mothers that touched our lives with encouragement all throughout our marriage.

Olevia Cogburn, Johnny's mother, on the left, and Ruth Patterson, Marilyn's mother, on the right.
(Photo from Cogburn family album)

Our mothers made our marriage stronger, and we still honor them. In addition, I honor my wife, who gave birth to our beautiful daughters Shelly, Leslie, and Rachel. It was on Mother's Day that year that I also presented Marilyn with a flower that was planted on the fence row of our new home. The flower was a perennial that bloomed in the spring year after year and never died. It was still blooming when we sold our home in April 2016. This was a sad day in our lives.

Memorial Day 2002 was fast approaching, and we had invited family and friends to join us for a cookout and to remember the sacrifice of all the men and women who made our nation's freedom possible.

As spring gave way to the summer heat, we occasionally took trips to Mt. Nebo and Petit Jean State Park, having a picnic and swim with family and friends.

Then summer gave way to fall. The nights got cooler and our porch became a place to enjoy the serenity of the night. This was a calm and peaceful getaway to collect our thoughts and just be still. Occasionally an owl sounded off in the distance and a coyote would howl. The moon shined light over our yard, and many times deer grazed after dark. The quietness Marilyn and I enjoyed still has a calming effect on me even though it was long ago.

The fall foliage ushered in magnificent colors, a beautiful time of year. Marilyn always wanted to get a pumpkin and a couple bales of hay to decorate the yard. This was an annual event. I so enjoyed helping her with any and all of the decorating. We noticed how the birds seemed to like our porch and the shelter it provided, so we bought birdfeeders and filled them with seeds. This really brought in all types of birds that we enjoyed watching through our picture window all year long. It was also time to begin gathering the seven ricks of wood for the winter months ahead. This process usually started in August and was completed by the first of November.

The first frosty morning, Marilyn had me build a fire in our fireplace, and then I boiled water on the stove for her hot chocolate, coffee for me, and breakfast. She fried bacon, putting homemade biscuits in the oven, getting eggs ready to be fried.

Oh, the aroma of wood burning, coffee perking, and bacon frying still whets my appetite. The memories of all those winter days we enjoyed and the times we spent together remain.

We followed this pattern throughout the winter months with the fire not only for its warmth but for the atmosphere. The popcorn that we shared and the smell that filtered all through the house while watching *CSI* (Marilyn's favorite show) and admiring the flames as they shadowed each side of the fireplace was comforting without a word being spoken. When the wind blew outside, you could hear it as though it was whispering words of a consoling nature, calming the mind of any troubling thoughts of the day.

Thanksgiving was about a month away. On many occasions we invited family and friends over to enjoy the smoked turkey and dressing, and the yeast rolls that were usually reserved for me to prepare and bake. Others brought their favorite dishes, and we all enjoyed a Thanksgiving feast. After the meal, we played board games or watched football. The day was spent relaxing and just being thankful for all the blessings the Lord provided, along with the memories of being together with family and friends.

After Thanksgiving, there were only a few short weeks before Christmas, and we had a lot of preparation before we were ready to host the next big holiday. Shopping for family and friends to get the right gifts and wrapping them neatly was such an important task for Marilyn. Next, the stockings for all our daughters and "grand dogs" had to be hung on our fireplace mantel in a row. The nine-foot Christmas tree had to be placed in front of our six-foot picture window. The decorations were hung with care just as Marilyn requested. The joy and happiness that we experienced at this stage of our lives was so rewarding. The cakes, cookies, candy, and especially the fudge—Marilyn made all with pleasure.

This first Christmas in our home would always be remembered for the blessings the Lord had bestowed on us and the details Marilyn and I worked on to make it the most enjoyable Christmas.

First Christmas in our dream home.
(Photos from Cogburn family album)

The next few years were enjoyed like the first with thankfulness, happiness, and contentment.

On February 28, 2005, Leslie gave birth to Myra, our first grandchild. Marilyn and I were such proud grandparents! We took to the role of spoiling our granddaughter. When we went to Walmart, she went with us. The toy section was her favorite. She would pick out a doll or toy of her liking, and we were more than happy to make the purchase.

Other places we enjoyed taking her were to family and friends' houses to celebrate birthdays and holiday parties. Our friends always gave her gifts and wanted to hold her. I even took Myra on my school bus route. She still remembers going with her Papa on his route. Marilyn had such a great time taking her shopping, buying her clothes and toys, and all the other things grandmothers do for their grandchildren. On her first birthday, she got cake all over her face, which was so funny.

Myra's first birthday. (Photo from the Cogburn family album)

Marilyn and I got much pleasure watching her grow. Myra's presence renewed feelings of closeness that we shared watching our daughters grow up.

As the years went by, we became more and more aware of the aches and pains that had become more frequent. I had arthroscopic knee surgery in 2007, and it took about two years to get back to somewhat normal. Marilyn had knee replacement surgery in 2010, which took much rehab for her to walk normally again. In 2012 we went to a Razorbacks game, and Marilyn got hot, passed out, fell, and broke her ankle. We both had more medical problems in a five-year span than during our entire lives. That was when we realized our health issues were becoming more and more frequent. We started talking about the possibility of selling our dream home, which I immediately dismissed. However, it would still come up, like being underwater and trying to get back to the surface to get enough oxygen to breathe. I just could not get my mind at peace whenever I thought of selling the home I'd built for Marilyn.

Even as health issues and decisions about selling our house

were on our minds, we found time to help at the church. In June 2013 our church was having a door-knocking campaign to invite kids to Vacation Bible school. At the time I was a bus driver for the school district. I knew most of the kids and their parents on my route, so Marilyn and I decided to invite many of those kids to VBS. This took place on a Saturday prior to the start of VBS. Marilyn and I went door to door introducing ourselves and asking parents if they would like their kids to attend VBS with us. We also informed them that we would pick them up in the church bus and bring them back home each day throughout the week. The last day of VBS, as a follow up, Marilyn and I asked the kids if they would like to continue going to church with us. Most went with their parents to other places on Sundays, but Wednesday evening Bible study was a great option for them and their parents.

We started picking them up in the church bus for Wednesday evening service. What a great opportunity for Marilyn and me to contribute some spiritual guidance to impoverished children whom we grew to love! The children ranged in age from four to twelve. Marilyn became very close to them and thought of them as her adopted children. She made sandwiches each time we picked them up for church. The sandwiches were nothing fancy, just PB&J with chips and a cookie. What a surprised look of thankfulness on the children's faces! The kids appreciated the kindness, sincerity, and love that we showed.

Forgetfulness and Change

In the summer of 2015, Marilyn was misplacing things in the house and not remembering their locations. At first it was not usually concerning, just noticeable. By September we decided to make an appointment with a neurologist. He did a brain scan, and we had to wait about a week before getting the results. The diagnosis was vascular dementia, a progressive form of Alzheimer's. The doctor described what he saw as the narrowing of the blood vessels that carry blood and oxygen to the brain. He explained it as a disease that is incurable and will result in a shortened life expectancy. This was devastating news! This incurable disease brought our future to a screeching halt. What were we to do? There was no cure for this progressive disease that would shorten Marilyn's life.

We were not ready to give up our dream home that had taken an immense amount of time, effort, and planning. Yet circumstances such as this disease charted the course for our future. I would not be able to take care of all the amenities that were created on our two-acre family property. We built an eleven hundred-square-foot house for our daughter, as well as an efficiency apartment we rented out. Now going forward, we must face Marilyn's health issues.

Our lives together, from the time we married in December 1970 until April 2015, were years of blessing. We had been so healthy and received mostly routine care with the exception of the previous five years. I had often stated if hospitals and physicians were waiting on us and people like us for their livelihood, they would have to get a second job. That being said, we were about to experience a dramatic change to our lives.

Thanksgiving 2015 would not be the same. Our will for

celebrating the season had been diminished by the news of our future. However long we assumed we had together had become shorter, and our thoughts focused on each other. I really did not think Marilyn understood all that was happening with the diagnosis and her life expectancy. I tried to shield her from any and all information related to her illness. We decided to have Christmas at our home, knowing this would probably be the last. We had all the usual family and friends over. Everyone enjoyed the day and the time spent together.

In January, my thoughts were still wrestling with the idea of selling our home. Marilyn had mainly left the decision up to me, a decision I did not want to make without her input. The long hours of labor that were put into building this home were still in the forefront of my mind. The sleepless nights, many of which I awoke in sweat and tears, not just for the place alone but for my wife whom I love dearly. The prayers I prayed were for Marilyn's health and for my spiritual guidance to make the best decisions going forward. What was I to do? This decision to sell or not to sell went on from January through March. After two months of praying and observing Marilyn's declining mental health, the decision was made to offer our place For Sale By Owner. I felt we would have more control of the process if the buyer came to us and offered on the asking price. The asking price would be nonnegotiable.

In March 2016, I placed a For Sale sign on the road that led to our home. I really did not think it would sell without the help of a real estate agent or the proper advertisement necessary to sell a house. A week passed when a couple showed up and inquired about our home. We welcomed them in and showed them room by room, detail after detail. The accents and features in the house that I worked so hard perfecting for my wife were selling points for this couple. They said they would get back to us after they talked about it. We thanked them for coming and did not think anything else of it, knowing it could take a while to get all the things together that are needed to purchase a house.

Then on Sunday, March 13, in the middle of the afternoon we received a call from that couple asking for another tour.

They wanted to show the rest of their family and get their opinion. This call came after a wonderful dinner of oven-fried chicken, creamed potatoes, pinto beans, biscuits, gravy, and brownies. This was a meal that brought back memories of when Marilyn invited a young coach from Magazine, Arkansas, to dinner with her parents a long time ago. It was also memorable because it would be the last unassisted meal Marilyn would make before her disease worsened.

When the couple came to tour the home, I had decided that my voice would remain silent and I'd let them take their family around. As I watched them, I realized they had more than just a passing interest. After the second tour was over, they informed us they were going to look into securing the financing and would keep in touch.

On the following Thursday, we received a phone call from a loan officer in Oregon representing the couple wanting to schedule an appraisal. I knew the appraisal had to be equal to our selling price, and if the loan officer did not come up with the asking price, then there would be other buyers. The call from the loan officer came on March 29, and the value of our home came in at $2,000 more than our asking price. This should have been welcome news, but it only brought anxious thoughts since we would be homeless in fewer than thirty days. I had turned seventy the October before and would never be able to build or replace a house at another location. We could have changed our minds, but I knew at this point the decision had already been made. The disease that was ravaging my wife made the decision to sell our home a little easier. I knew I still needed to provide for her even if it meant giving up our dream home.

April 28 at two o'clock, the closing documents would be signed. Questions surfaced that begged for answers, such as: Will we find a place within our budget? We still had to pack the house and search for a new home. I became anxious to start the search for a home in Fayetteville, Arkansas, where my daughter and granddaughter lived. We began our search for something to rent because of the short timeframe. After looking at several places to lease, we did not find anything we felt comfortable renting. We wanted a place of our own.

Our daughter Leslie chauffeured us around town and offered advice on where to live. I became stressed because every house we looked at was either too expensive or not acceptable. Marilyn was okay with whatever decision that was made. I again had second thoughts about selling our home.

On April 3, after stopping at Braum's for lunch, Marilyn asked me to pass her the sports section of the newspaper. I began looking at the classifieds under the housing section to see if there were any houses for sale. After skimming through the paper, I was about to put it away when I noticed an ad that said For Sale By Owner. I asked Leslie if she knew the location, and she said it was not far from her house. We located the house, and from every indication, this looked like it might be the place. We called and made an appointment to tour the home. After the tour, we decided to make an offer, which they accepted and sold us the home. This was good news for us because now we would be able to make our final plans to move.

On Thursday, April 28, 2016, we turned the final page of a chapter in our lives that will long be remembered. We got up early and watched the sunrise for the last time from our front porch, a view we had experienced countless times. The memories that were created here of days and years past are still so clear in my mind: the first night we spent in our home and the warmth of the open fire, Marilyn's retirement party at her sister's house with cake, a money tree, and a gathering of friends and family. Also, among those memories are Marilyn's mother, Ruth, who always had a "large time" when she came for a visit, and my mother, Olevia, who spent time swinging with me on our porch swing. Other memories include throwing snowballs at each other as we gathered the drifting snow to make ice cream, the popcorn we shared while sitting in front of the fireplace watching television, the birds that we enjoyed watching through our picture window, and the quiet times we spent on our porch reminiscing. The swimming parties, the birthday parties, and holiday parties are memories filled with laughter. Our granddaughter celebrated her first birthday here—complete with cake on her face. The deer grazing in our front yard late in the evening, the homecooked meals Marilyn and I prepared together, the stews, chili, cornbread, and cobblers enjoyed with family and friends are all treasured memories. I remember the baby owl that lost its way and perched on our porch, the prayers that were prayed, the tears that were shed when our parents passed away, and the reading of the Bible together.

Before we began this new chapter, I looked back on the pages of time to the very beginning, after Marilyn and I were married. We had gone to her parents' house where she lived and loaded everything she owned into her car so she could move into a rented mobile home with me. The furnishings were a bed, a chair, and some plastic forks and spoons. My pocketknife doubled as a kitchen knife when needed. What else did a coach need? I was never home anyway. Someone gave us a couch and a second chair. Our television was at Walmart; it just had not been purchased yet. What we brought to the home was good health and good jobs. Our world was simple. We lived within our means, stayed close, and depended on each other.

As I looked around our present home and all the things we had accumulated, it was amazing to me how much stuff we had collected over the years. The sight was overwhelming! Though many of our possessions had sentimental value, they would have to be sold because the house we were moving to was smaller. So we decided to have an estate sale. After the sale, we still had more furnishings than we wanted to take with us, so we decided to hire a local auction company to sell the rest of the things we no longer wanted. The results were more than half our belongings liquidated, making the move easier.

After the sales were over, we had ten days to vacate the property. How do you close the door on a home that was built with personal time, labor, and patience for a woman I had prayed for and met at the gym in Magazine, Arkansas, so many years ago? Our world centered around each other.

Oh! What would I do if only I could? I would bring back another day of the past that only seems like yesterday. I would turn back the pages of time to March 14, 2002, and relive the happiness and joy we once knew. I would ask time to stand still and allow us to live as if there were no tomorrows, only this day.

If only I could! I even had a conversation with Time. "Mr. Time, if you could talk, what would you say to me?"

He responded, "Mankind gauges all their lives and activities around me. They plan for the future as if they will be present to fulfill plans that were made. The human race is frantically searching for ways and means to gain material wealth. I grant you only the present. I will continue into the future although you may not be there yourself. I have been taken for granted by man. Man simply does not understand who I am. My presence is everywhere. Though you cannot see me, you can experience my being here. I myself have an endless amount of time to offer in order to accomplish those futile goals. The only problem is that man only has a fixed amount of time to accomplish whatever he may be trying to achieve."

"I never regress to the past," I answered. "Mr. Time, can you be stopped?"

"*No!* Sometimes humans only wish I could. I have given you a day-to-day schedule to meet. When you were in your youth, you thought very little of how time was spent as you were always looking to the future and the next enjoyable occasion. As you grew older and realized that you are now in the autumn years, you started to look back at the spring of your life, which now I have taken away."

"Mr. Time! I want to ask you a personal question. What happens when one's lifelong mate passes, and the one left has the task of trying to cope with a gaping hole that will never be filled by another? The hole may be patched over, but never filled."

"I can only refer you to Ecclesiastes 3:1–8, which best describes me as having 'every purpose under heaven.'"

"Mr. Time, what conclusion, then, can be drawn from my conversation with you?"

"Man's time spent upon this earth is limited. Let's consider time as being the hub of a wheel. Everything revolves around the hub. What gift is more important to man's existence than time?"

This is the question that I ask myself as I look back on all the work and time that was sacrificed that could have been put to use doing other things. My thoughts returned to the years spent with my parents and the time they invested in me, showing by example that strong work ethics, applied with good common sense can achieve goals you set for yourself. Was it all worth it? Yes! It was worth giving my labor and time for a woman who loved and cared for me, a woman who never complained and was always happy in the present.

She never wanted an extravagant lifestyle, only a life filled with the simple joy of family, friends, and a husband whom she loved in a life filled with devotion. We took pictures of each other from our porch facing the west where we watched the sunset behind Mount Nebo each day. We said our final goodbyes to a place that will always be remembered as being built for a woman named ... **Marilyn.**

The Move, and Life in Fayetteville

In May 2016 we settled into the home we'd purchased in a nice middle-class neighborhood in Fayetteville. We got acquainted with a few of our neighbors. Everyone gave us a warm and friendly welcome to the subdivision.

Marilyn liked her new home and neighborhood. Though she was unable to drive our car, she was still able to do laundry, write checks, and pay bills. As the year progressed, those tasks became more difficult. By 2017, she voluntarily turned those tasks over to me. As the year passed, I continued to notice the slow and gradual changes occurring in my wife's mental function. Simple tasks she was able to do a few months earlier were becoming harder to complete. In the meantime, we had to prepare for our youngest daughter's wedding.

During the preparation for the wedding, Rachel had a memorable experience to share about her mother. This is the story told to me by Rachel of her mother, Marilyn, preparing for Rachel's wedding:

> Two years into my mom's diagnosis (2017), she became fixated on one thing at a time and would not let it go until it was resolved. In the planning of my wedding, my mom was so worried about what she was going to wear; however, shopping for long periods of time and trying on dresses wasn't really an option with her attention span. Luckily, a friend came to the rescue and picked out a couple of options for her. We settled on one, and the friend altered it to fit Mom's size. Issue resolved.
>
> Well, the next thing I know, I'm getting phone call after phone call from her worried about

shoes. "What shoes should I wear? Will you take me shopping for shoes? What if I don't have shoes for the wedding?"

"It's all going to be okay, Mom. We'll go shopping soon."

Shopping day was here, and I took her to Dillard's. I frantically walked around the store corralling her, trying not to let her out of my sight, while still pulling shoes off the shelf and giving them to the department store clerk to pull her size from the backroom. I stumbled upon a shoe style that she enjoyed wearing in the past. They were black, sparkly, ballet style that crisscrossed around her ankles and had enough support for her not to lose them while dancing, which was her new way to express her happiness and newly acquired carefree attitude.

The clerk brought out the perfect size, and I helped her put them on. It was absolute magic when she put them on her feet, so much so that she started snapping her fingers and dancing around the Dillard's shoe department. I watched in embarrassment for a moment. Then I let down my guard, snapped, sang, and danced with her, and at that moment, I knew what it was like to be as carefree as she was in those moments. I never saw my mom sing and dance like this when I was growing up, but this horrific, mind-altering disease left her and me with a newfound attitude, new ways to express herself now that her mind wouldn't allow her to put nouns and verbs together in sentences to communicate.

The day, October 28, 2017, arrived quickly. Our youngest daughter, Rachel, was to be given away in marriage by me in a few short minutes to a wonderful guy named Matt Tracy. When we, her parents, saw our last child enter marriage, there was much happiness for our daughter and future son-in-law. As parents, giving away our baby daughter in marriage reminds us that this joyous moment comes once in a lifetime; yet the moment brings back memories of when Rachel was a baby girl, dragging her pink security blanket around the house, and the times Marilyn and I sat on the floor with her playing dolls. Then there was her first rocking horse, the first tricycle, her first bicycle, and all the T-ball games, softball games, and watching her hit home runs. Now it was her chance to collect memories with Matt in their new life together.

Rachel's wedding. From left to right: Myra Baugh, Leslie Cogburn, Rachel Tracy, Matt Tracy, Marilyn Cogburn, and Johnny Cogburn. (Photo courtesy of Two Carters Photography)

Following the wedding ceremony, there was a reception for family and friends. The dinner was a more formal setting while dress was more informal. After dinner, when Rachel and I had our father/daughter dance, many thoughts of her as a little girl swirled through my mind. She was so beautiful. Marilyn and I had just given away our baby daughter in marriage. I asked myself, where did the years go? The happiness we shared has given way to a future where my wife can no longer communicate well enough for me to understand her. This was a chapter of our lives together that was fast coming to an end. Frank Sinatra sang a song called "Once upon a Time Never Comes Again." This song reflects how we were in the early years of our lives, and those years have turned into memories.

At the Attorney's Office in Danville

We arrived in Danville on February 12, 2018, and parked a short distance from the attorney's office. So many memories and friendships were made here, such as Marilyn's childhood, our lives here together in the early 1980s, the births of two of our daughters (Shelly and Leslie), and my student teaching.

One notable memory while doing my student teaching was the time my Volkswagen disappeared from the school parking lot. One afternoon my car was no longer in its spot. I frantically searched and eventually found it around the corner and down the street from the school. Who could be responsible for this thievery? I spoke to the assistant coach about the strange new location of my vehicle. He immediately suspected who the culprits could be. Who would have thought teenage girls could have conspired and put forth the effort to push a VW Bug several hundred feet down the road to play a prank, instead of using that energy constructively in class? Since school was already out and all the kids had gone home, the assistant coach informed me we would have a meeting in the morning with the girls to discuss this matter. However, there would be a surprise waiting for them.

Students hiding the intern coach's car.
(Illustration by Myra Baugh)

The next morning when it was time for class, the assistant coach called for the girls' PE class to meet in the gym. He had spoken with the local police deputy about the situation, and together they had devised a plan to scare these girls straight. The deputy would stay in the dressing room until he was called on, and the girls would be in for quite a surprise.

After they were seated, the assistant coach and I spoke one at a time about the seriousness of moving someone's car without permission and how it could be considered theft of property and lead to jail time. When we were done with our lecture, he brought the deputy out, and the girls' facial expressions changed from one of boredom to one of guilt. Not knowing what their fate might be after the deputy informed them of the seriousness of the act, he told them he would leave the decision up to intern teacher, Mr. Cogburn, whether to pursue criminal charges. I had no intention of filing charges, but the girls didn't know that. Instead, I waited a few days to see how they responded. The assistant coach, the deputy, and I had a good laugh, and the looks on their faces made our day.

I cannot speak for the girls, but I am fairly certain they were not thinking of pushing a Volkswagen Bug off the parking lot anymore.

Although those memories of good laughter are cherished, the seriousness of the present weighed on me. I would have preferred the day to be one of leisure than business. My thoughts should have been focused on enjoying the day with Marilyn, reminiscing those fond memories made here before and after we married. Memories such as going to the theater and watching *Love Story* and *Patton*, both highly acclaimed movies of the day. On occasion, Marilyn talked about those fun times spent with friends going to the movies. Some of those friends would join us for lunch after we met with the attorney.

Our meeting with the attorney had been postponed for several months. Now that meeting was only minutes away. As I held Marilyn's hand and we approached the door to the lobby, a calm yet empty feeling came over me. It was a feeling of helplessness knowing she was about to give power of attorney to me. We sat in the lobby and waited about five minutes before we met with the attorney. Then we exchanged pleasantries. The attorney was one of Marilyn's former students.

He sat down and asked Marilyn questions, such as, "Do you understand what you are here for?" He then asked if I would like to explain to Marilyn why we were here. I declined, so he explained very meticulously all the subheadings in the document she would be signing.

When all the questions were asked and answered, the attorney asked, "Do you give your husband power of attorney over you?"

She said yes. I felt her deep abiding confidence and love for me in transferring the possessions we jointly held and all future decisions to be made on her behalf to me. I felt that I had been dreaming and woke up in the attorney's office to the realization that this was not imagined, and our lives would not be the same from this day forward.

Since leaving the attorney's office, my thoughts reflected on the legal contract Marilyn signed. I just could not wrap my head around what was happening to our lives. The disease that had befallen my wife was no dream and would not go away. I immediately asked myself how I would be able to make decisions on her behalf and not feel guilty about them. What happened from this day forward can only be known by spiritual powers, of which I pleaded with for help.

On our way home, we passed by Mount Magazine and took pictures of the ice and snow from a distance. I stood next to a woman—my wife and our children's mother—who had placed her confidence and total care of her well-being in my hands. Our future and the future decisions I would make on her behalf weighed heavily on my mind. I asked myself why she was the one that got sick and not me. Was this divine selection or was this the way the Lord had chosen to challenge me and my spiritual endurance? What was I going to do? This was my beloved wife, whom I had prayed for before we met and had been with for forty-seven years. The weight of my new responsibility lay heavily upon my shoulders, the responsibility I must accept for the care of my wife in sickness and in health.

I no longer thought of my wife as an adult but rather as a

child to care for and protect and to see after her needs, which meant putting my needs aside. It was my prayer that the Lord would guide me in the care of my loved one. *May God, through the Spirit, guide me in making the right decisions.* God answered my prayers in giving me a wife as a helpmate for all those years, and now I was to see after her needs since she was no longer able to take care of herself.

The Day-to-Day Struggle with Change and Loneliness

Valentine's Day 2018 began with presenting Marilyn a bouquet of flowers. Next we had breakfast, did some shopping, and then ate at another of our favorite restaurants. For lunch, Marilyn ordered chicken noodle soup and coconut pie. We had a pleasant time together. As I looked across the table at my lovely wife, I studied the expression on her face, but what I saw was a stare of emptiness. As we ate, there was no conversation, only a sense of urgency to finish the meal. All in all, the meal and the time together went smoothly. Even though there wasn't much conversation, we were still able to enjoy the quietness of being together, and that made it a good day.

Marilyn never mentioned having a Valentine's card for me and that was fine. I never expected anything from her because of her mental condition. I did not even think she was aware of the holiday. A few days later I found a note folded and left on the top of her dresser in our bedroom. She did not give it to me in person, as if she wanted me to find it. The note read, "I love you Johnny."

The Valentine Note. (Written by Marilyn Cogburn for Johnny)

How touching! A passing thought at that time made her want to write it down to remember later. That note is now next to her picture, which I look at every night.

The change in my wife was even more noticeable today. She did not know how to eat or use the bathroom. She was confused and simply did not understand things.

I wondered, *Where has my patience gone? How am I going to keep my sanity? How do I deal with all the guilt that I feel? When Marilyn looks into my eyes, what does she see? Does she see a husband who loves her or a husband who has shielded himself from a mental illness that could befall him?*

My wife asked me yesterday and again today if I loved her. She must want to be reassured that my love for her has not changed since we exchanged vows.

March 16 I woke at six. The day began as usual, although when I looked out the window, an eerie feeling came over me. The sky was dark and looked like rain. The gloominess of the sky seemed to parallel my feelings that something bad was about to happen. I knew this day would come, but when?

In September 2015, Marilyn was diagnosed with vascular dementia, a progressive form of Alzheimer's. The neurologist said it was incurable. Medication could help slow the progression, but the outcome would remain the same.

Marilyn's symptoms took a dramatic turn today. What does this all mean? As her husband, this was devastating. I had been caring for her needs. The burden was getting mentally and physically heavy. The separation after forty-seven years had become real!

Two women from church had scheduled a lunch visit with Marilyn today at eleven. The women ate and had a good visit talking and laughing together. After the women said their goodbyes, Marilyn announced that she wanted to go into town but not for any particular reason; she just wanted to go somewhere.

When I asked her if there was somewhere specific, she replied, "I don't know, uptown?"

I didn't know where to go or what she wanted to do. I just knew she wanted to go somewhere. So with that in mind I decided to take her to Gulley Park, which was not far from our home. I thought we could walk a while, sit on the benches, watch the birds and squirrels, and admire the beautiful buttercups.

When I stopped the car and started to get out, Marilyn said, 'I don't want to go to the park." She got very angry with me. Her mind-set and my thought process had just arrived on a collision course.

I felt the need to get help. I had previously talked with the administrator at Fayetteville Health and Rehab about long-term care, so I decided to take her there and follow up on our conversation. When we arrived, the administrator immediately knew we needed help. After talking briefly, she wanted us to go to Vantage Point and follow her in our vehicle.

When we arrived, I was given a three-page questionnaire to fill out on Marilyn's personal and medical history. After completing all the forms, we began the waiting process to see someone for an interview for admittance to the facility. All the while we were waiting, Marilyn never understood the purpose of why we were there. This was very difficult for me. My wife, whom I love dearly, was about to be admitted to the psychiatric unit of Vantage Point. I felt so much pain as we sat waiting for the interview. My brain was about to explode with guilt. *Why am I admitting my wife to a facility that will be a permanent separation for us?*

I had to go back and review my thoughts and ask the reason we were here in the first place. I simply could no longer provide the twenty-four hours a day, seven days a week care that my wife needed.

After waiting about fifteen minutes, a male nurse came in and introduced himself and began the process. An attendant holding my wife's arm escorted her down the long hallway. As she left my side, frightened, tears flowing down her cheeks, she looked over her shoulder at me and vanished as the sound of locking doors echoed down the long hallway. I watched in sadness; my heart flooded with grief. I was reminded of the apostle Peter's denial of Christ. When Christ was led away, he turned and looked back at Peter (see Luke 22:61 for more information).[2] The parallel imagery of betrayal was resting squarely on my shoulders. It was like a scene from a horror movie as my spouse was being taken against her will, and as her husband, I could not help her. This was all happening before my eyes; that echoing sound of locking doors can still be heard. The sound was a reminder of the separation that will come with the finality of her life.

I was now standing alone looking down an empty hallway waiting on an attendant to open the exit door. *What have I just done?* Silence had engulfed me. I had just turned my wife over to unknown caregivers. This was completely out of character. Nothing like this had ever happened to us in our lifetime. We had been close and protective of each other since we married, but now my decision to admit her to this facility was in question. The burden of guilt I felt was overwhelming. On the way home, my mind searched for a solution to a problem that is impossible in human terms to solve.

When I arrived home and went to bed, sleep evaded me. My mind was in a state of shock. The very thought that there is no medical cure for this disease was so painful. My thoughts had entirely turned to the spiritual realm for future guidance for my loved one.

On Sunday, March 18, visitation was from ten to eleven a.m. I arrived at Vantage Point at 9:55. I walked down the same long hallway that Marilyn had walked and through the two security doors. Marilyn was waiting. The final door locked behind me and before I could sit, she immediately insisted I take her home. The attendant had to step between us to avoid a confrontation, and I had to leave early. Guilt had overtaken me; I was still feeling remorse for her being there to begin with. Now to leave under these circumstances, rejection, and the feeling of being alone to live with the pain of my decision weighed on me.

A couple of days later, I debated whether I should visit Marilyn. The last visit had made me more concerned about future visits. I asked myself, *If I go, will today's outcome be the same as the day before?* It did not take long to make that decision, and I am glad I went. Rachel went with me, and we had a good visit with Marilyn. Because she was unable to stay still, Marilyn walked and paced with anxiety most of the time we were there. The attendant did not have to intervene, and we did not have to leave early.

On Easter Sunday, I arrived at Vantage Point at 9:45 with Bible in hand to read Luke 24 to Marilyn and pray with her. After my visit, I went to eat with my family in Bentonville. Before the meal, I spoke for myself and on behalf of Marilyn. The meal was on us as a blessing to our family. The prayer before the meal was so emotional that it was hard for me to complete without becoming tearful. The lunch was delicious, and the time spent with my daughters, son-in-law, and grandchild was good for me. Throughout the meal, I felt the emptiness in the seat beside me that I only began to feel within the past few weeks. Before that, Marilyn had always been by my side. At the end of the meal, everyone thanked Marilyn and me for our blessing.

The Monday after Easter, I received a call from Vantage Point saying Marilyn would be discharged and taken to Fayetteville Health and Rehab April 3. This was good news!

We family members and Marilyn would have more freedom for visits. I welcomed the freedom to eat meals and sit with her. This helped me fill in time that previously was spent alone!

The time I got to spend with my wife now had taken on a challenge that in human terms was hard to define. Her spoken words were becoming difficult to understand. My role as her husband went from the traditional one of being the breadwinner, head of household, and husband to one of a parent trying to communicate and take care of an adult with the mind of a three-year-old.

By Sunday, April 8, the mental fatigue overwhelmed me. I had a good night's sleep but woke to an emptiness. My wife, who had shared the other half of my bed, was not there anymore. I cried out for her, yet my cry was only met with silence. *Where is my partner? Why is she no longer by my side? How can such a disease be so cruel as to come between a husband and a wife and leave such a void?*

This was a never-ending struggle that faced me daily. Loneliness was like a stranger I had befriended. Afterward, I expected him to be on his way. Instead, he stalked me, and his presence was felt wherever I went. He constantly reminded me of his existence and what he represented. The thought of being alone kept coming back to mind. Webster's Dictionary defines loneliness as the "unfulfilled desire for another's company." The first recorded description of loneliness is found in Genesis 2:18.

The unwelcome stranger returned as a ghostly reminder of past nights spent alone. The last few years of my coaching career were spent on the road during the week and home on the weekends. When I came home, Marilyn would be there waiting with outstretched arms, ready to welcome her husband. The loneliness we felt being away from each other during that time would be nothing compared to the loneliness I felt knowing my wife would not be coming home. Those temporary nights of the past spent alone had now become permanent.

My personal description of loneliness as it relates to the husband/wife relationship is that each is a part of a whole, but now one part has been taken away. Loneliness is the absence of the smile I love, the facial expressions that are unseen, the laughter that once gave me pleasure to be around, the companion that gave consolation when I was sad, the absence of dinner at our favorite restaurants, the curious stares as I sit alone at a table or booth, and the holidays I'd once looked forward to.

These were now filled with emptiness because my companion was no longer able to share them with me. Loneliness, the unwelcome stranger, was now my faithful companion. My conclusion was that time was the only medicine to accept. It is not a cure, but only a resolve to move forward and leave the past for the present. This is not as difficult for some as it is for others. We are not all wired the same. The timeline for some may be shorter while others may take longer to sort out the past before moving to the present.

Monday, April 9, was another day of change in Marilyn because of her combativeness with another resident and the staff. She would have to go back to the psychiatric unit at Vantage Point, a more confined facility, to get her behavior and medications regulated.

According to Forrest Gump's mother, "Life is like a box of chocolates; you never know what you're going to get." The road of life is not easy. Our choices can make a difference. Avoiding potholes is a challenge. Nevertheless, the unexpected can happen to anyone, and time has a way of shortening the space between the unexpected and the end of life. When we were in our early twenties, just beginning our careers and lives together, the very thought of our lives ending was not concerning. Though at some point we knew it would end, yet we were not worried. It was old people who died, not us.

Marilyn in her current condition shocked me. I didn't think of her as being old. To me, she was still that young woman who walked into my life through those double doors of the gym in Magazine. I was still trying to come to grips with my thoughts after fifteen months of visiting and seeing her daily while in the nursing home. My thoughts played a cruel trick on me in believing she was only in the nursing home for a period of time and then after she was well enough, I would be able to take her home and our life would return to normal.

Yogi Berra once said, "When you come to a fork in the road, just take it." This fork in the road became a dead end. There was no other route, no best choice. All the routes and choices led straight to this dead end. There was no U-turn. Oh, how I wish there was! The disease was taking her life on a slow downward spiral of which there was no return. I remember a quote from an unknown author: "The best of me is gone." These words clearly described the feeling of helplessness and the invisible road ahead we all must travel, though some sooner than others.

When two lives are joined together for forty-seven years and one is separated from the other and placed in a nursing facility, how is the other partner's behavior defined? How much time should be spent with the spouse at the facility? Should most of the time be spent there, or should there be some type of compromising balance? This was new and uncharted territory for me. *Does it really matter what other people think? Yes, it matters to me.* I felt the need for public support and approval from friends and family. The feeling of isolation from others became noticeable, especially when I was asked about Marilyn. The asking seemed to occur less often, and my presence was more isolated.

How was I to break from a bond that was interwoven between the spiritual and physical, a bond that took years to cultivate? The apostle Paul wrote in Romans 8:35–39, "Who can separate us from the love of Christ?" It is certain death will separate us from our earthly physical bond that we share. That said, Marilyn and I shared a spiritual bond in Christ that will last forever.

On Saturday, April 18, I visited Marilyn around three thirty in the afternoon. I brought her a chocolate shake and some Hershey's candy. She was asleep when I arrived. I kissed her cheek.

She said, "I'm so glad to see you, and I've been thinking about you."

The closeness of the moment was heartfelt. My wife and partner are never far from my thoughts. When I woke this morning, thoughts of Marilyn by my side were so real. I felt her when I looked around our bedroom and saw her picture by our bedside. As I walked into the hallway and saw the family pictures on display, each one with a tie to a special time in our lives, I felt her presence. The pictures showed us when we were young and the world was ours to enjoy. All the memories in our house, everywhere I looked, reminded me of a woman who took great care and pride in all things that turn a house into a home.

When Marilyn woke, we held hands and walked to the patio area of the facility. I tried to steer the conversation about things that should have been easy for her to remember, such as our retirement home in Dardanelle, the church bus ministry that was part of our lives for two years, outings at Mt. Nebo State Park, or holidays with family. This was one way for me to test her memory.

Today, unlike previous days, she was not able to remember that we even lived in Dardanelle. This was sad for me because conversations about our past were a way to communicate and connect with her. It was a way for me to feel that closeness we shared in the retirement home that was built for her.

When I arrived at Vantage Point for a visit on Sunday, April 15, Marilyn was so glad to see me. We held hands and had conversation. Most of Marilyn's conversation was unintelligible, but I understood the words, "I love you." Nothing else really mattered. The eye contact, the tears that flowed down our cheeks, and the silence of the moment communicated the love we have for each other. Just being together was enough. We spent the visit holding hands and exchanging facial expressions. It was as though Marilyn was aware of the other world in which she once lived but now was no longer able to function or communicate in.

I arrived at the facility around 4:45 on April 26. One of the caretakers said Marilyn had been looking for me. When I went to her room, I found her in a deep sleep. After I woke her, we went outside to the patio where we had dinner. We tried to talk but no words were understood, and conversation was decreasing with each passing day.

The next day, I arrived at the facility around 4:50 and found Marilyn again sound asleep. When I woke her, she hugged my neck, and I asked her if she wanted to go to dinner. She declined, indicating she just wanted to go back to sleep. The medicine she had been taking was causing her to sleep most of the day. After a while I convinced her to get up and go to dinner.

When she got up, she picked up the family picture album that was on display on her dresser. There were individual pictures of family members taken over the years. She carried the photo album to the dining room, and with her face beaming, she showed the other residents pictures of her family. She finally brought the album to the patio area where she would eat her first meal of puréed food. Instead of setting the album down while we ate, she got up and took the album back inside and showed off the pictures again. It was so sad to observe how far my wife's memory had declined. This was her way of expressing her love for her family to others. These pictures represented the only connection she had to the outside world.

On Sunday, April 29, I received a call from Fayetteville Health and Rehab that Marilyn had fallen and landed on her right hip. They had already called EMS to transport her to Washington Regional Medical Center. I went to the facility as soon as I could. I met the ambulance as they arrived. The emergency responders placed Marilyn on a stretcher and took her to the hospital. After the exam and X-rays, the result was she had fractured her hip in three different places. She would need surgery the following Monday, April 30.

That day, Marilyn went into surgery around 11:30, which only lasted thirty minutes, and the doctor came to the waiting room to report to Rachel and me that all went well. The doctor said a rod was placed in her leg and a full recovery was expected. He said she should be able to walk again after rehab. He also said she would be in recovery in the hospital for three or four days.

That day, she slept most of the afternoon and did not eat or drink much. Rachel and Matt stayed until 8:15 p.m. when I came to relieve them. She continued to sleep until around 10 p.m., and then she tried to get out of bed. I called for help and four nurses came to settle her down. They gave her medicine to calm her, and she finally fell asleep. She was still sleeping when I left at midnight.

The next day, I arrived at the hospital around 10:15 a.m. A therapist was trying to get Marilyn up for therapy, but she was not cooperating. Since she was not willing to help him, there was little he could do.

Marilyn was released from the hospital May 2 and transported back to Fayetteville Health and Rehab. The therapist immediately tried to start the therapy process, but Marilyn was once again not cooperating.

When I arrived at the nursing home around 6:45 p.m. on Wednesday, May 9, I walked down the long hallway to her room and saw that her door was closed. When I tried opening it, I found something was blocking it. When I pushed the door open, I saw Marilyn lying on the floor. My heart raced as I checked to see if she was okay. Her eyes were open, and she was looking around. I called for help and the nurses quickly helped me get her back into bed. Then Marilyn went back to sleep.

My wife was injured and did not understand that her leg was broken. This disease destroyed her ability to think and reason. This was concerning to me. My wife went from walking down the hall with me to dinner to not wanting to walk or get out of bed within a four-day period. The nursing home scheduled an appointment with the psychiatrist later that evening. I met with him for two hours, and he explained what could be expected for my wife's care going forward. After that lengthy conversation with the doctor, I felt there was no other choice but to admit her to hospice care. This was a most difficult decision for me. This meant there would be no therapist for rehab to help her learn to walk again. She would be confined to a bed and wheelchair for the rest of her life.

The next day I arrived at the facility around 10:48 a.m. Five of Marilyn's close friends came with me. Marilyn was glad to see them all. What a blessing to have such friends who have stayed close throughout the years! We got an attendant to help Marilyn get out of bed and into a wheelchair, and we went out to the patio to visit and have lunch.

Sunday, May 13, was Mother's Day. This was a day for reflection and to give thanks for all mothers, past and present. For those of us who can remember, we may think of our childhood with our mothers wiping tears from our eyes or the embrace and hugs they gave no matter the circumstances. Maybe we remember our mother's tearful eyes after we came home to visit as adults or the phone conversations where she just wanted to hear the voice of the child she loves.

Not knowing what world my wife was in when she cried out for her mother made my mind wonder what she could have needed from her. What was she asking for? The comforting hugs of her mother from long ago, or reassuring words in her present state of being?

Our daughters and I arrived at the nursing home around 12:15, and we took Marilyn to the patio area and had lunch. Marilyn was alert and recognized everyone. We stayed until two when Marilyn was ready for her afternoon nap.

On May 22 I arrived at the nursing home around five, and Marilyn was already in the dining room. She was asleep in her wheelchair with her food getting cold on the tray in front of her. I sat by the window and observed. After an hour, the staff tried to wake her so she could eat. She only ate a few bites and responded very little, never opening her eyes. She was taken back to her room and put to bed.

When I arrived the next day, Marilyn was once again asleep in her wheelchair in the dining room. This time, however, she woke up and recognized me immediately. She hugged and kissed me while saying, "Johnny! Johnny! Johnny! I love you."

This got the attention of everyone around us. For me this was a tranquil and solemn moment in time. To see those beautiful brown eyes staring at me and expressing from the heart her feelings of joy and love for me was a gift that I will cherish always.

On Sunday, May 27, I attended church and afterward went to visit Marilyn. Rachel and Leslie came as well. We had lunch together and Marilyn held Rachel's hand while praying a heartfelt prayer. Though the words were unintelligible, the spiritual realm would be able to interpret. We all prayed together with thankfulness, and I got a sense of her accepting the reality of a life after death.

She mentioned heaven on two separate occasions, today

being one. The word in itself is beautiful, coupled with the thought of being prepared and wanting to go there makes the word even more beautiful.

Again, I arrived at the facility around lunchtime on Thursday, June 2. Marilyn was in her wheelchair in the TV area, crying. A nurse who was helping her informed me that she had slept until eleven o'clock and had just been given her medicine.

I put my arms around her, and she responded with a hug and a kiss. This was one of those moments where I felt a connection to her that was extremely touching. It was as though her hugging me and crying triggered a flashback of memories, as though she felt helpless and was begging and pleading with me for help. Help that I was unable to give. She was not in any pain. Her intellect was trying to transmit information to me, but her words were not being understood. I have a picture of Marilyn as a little girl in our living room, and the innocence that the picture portrays is the closeness that I have always felt to that little girl who now is my wife. The world that she once knew was taken away by a disease that has no limitations.

On Saturday, June 16 and that past week, Leslie spent time with her mother. She and Myra, our granddaughter, would be moving to California for a new start. We wished them the best with our love.

When I arrived on Friday, June 29, again around lunchtime, I brought Marilyn's uncle and his wife. Marilyn held his hand and they simulated keeping time with the music. I think he played out long before Marilyn.

Saturday, July 21 was a good day. Marilyn was eating dinner in the dining room. After she finished, I took her to the lobby and talked to her of things from our past, such as swinging on the porch swing, eating popcorn in front of the fireplace, Christmas and the gifts exchanged, and meals we prepared for family and friends. Tears started flowing down her cheeks. We embraced, and I could no longer hold back my own tears. For a moment, something I said triggered a memory of the past, shared moments that we relished.

August 25 was another memorable day. I arrived at the nursing home around 12:15 p.m. Marilyn was in the dining room in her wheelchair waiting for lunch. When she saw me, she wanted to give me a hug. I bent down, and we embraced and kissed.

She cried as we embraced and then asked me, "What have you been doing?"

I felt a sense of her wanting to be part of whatever I had been doing. She knew I was doing something that she was once a part of and had shared. I felt pain as she looked into my eyes. She had been so active her entire life and enjoyed her freedom, but now she was confined to her bed or wheelchair. For me to watch and feel the frustration and mental torture that I knew she felt was heartbreaking.

The lyrics in one of Jim Reeves's songs best defines my life going forward. The song is "I Can't Stop Loving You," and the line I relate to is, "It's useless to say so I just live my life in dreams of yesterday."

Today I visited Marilyn around 11:20. She was already in the dining room waiting for lunch. She usually got her lunch tray around 12:20. I sat in a chair next to her and waited with her. When her tray was brought to the table, I fed her. She played with a teddy bear the whole time.

After she ate about three fourths of her meal, she dropped her teddy bear and focused her attention on me. Until that moment she had not realized I had been feeding her. As we embraced, she cried tears of thankfulness for me, which was timeless within itself. It was as though she knew in her helpless state that her lifelong partner was there at her side to comfort, console, and be there for her. This inward feeling is indescribable.

When I arrived around 11:30 on Friday morning, Marilyn was still asleep in bed. The staff had gotten her up for breakfast, said she ate well, and then put her back to bed. Around 11:45 the staff woke her and dressed her in a Razorback pullover, placed her in her wheelchair, and brought her to the television area.

Today was her birthday; she turned seventy. She was born on Monday, August 30, 1948. She received cards from her friends, which I read to her. She briefly cried. Marilyn's sisters called to wish her a happy birthday. I brought her a cake, which we shared with the staff. Our pictures were taken, and the staff sang "Happy Birthday" to her. I pushed her wheelchair to the dining room where I fed her. She ate her meal and had a cup of pureed birthday cake for dessert. After her meal she fell asleep in her wheelchair.

Later that day around 5:00, Rachel, Matt and I came for an evening visit. After we visited and had dinner, she was taken to the TV area and fell asleep watching TV.

September 8, 2018, was the Walk to End Alzheimer's and also Rachel's birthday. I arrived in Bentonville, Arkansas, around 9:30 a.m. to participate in the race. Rachel Tracy was designated to be the family team captain. Our team theme is "Stepping out for Marilyn." Many of our family members walked the one-mile course. Our goal was to raise $1,500 to help with research in finding a cure for this terrible disease. There were many friends and family members who could not be present but contributed online to support and help us reach our goal, which we exceeded! We celebrated Rachel's birthday at lunch.

During the race, around ten o'clock, I received a call from the nursing home. We had only walked about a third of the course at this time. My anxiety level rose. The nurse informed me that Marilyn had fallen out of her wheelchair and onto the concrete floor. She had landed on her right side and hit her head on the floor.

The nurse followed up by saying, "She seems to be okay, but there is a red spot on the side of her face."

The nurse said they were monitoring her closely and would let me know if she needed follow-up treatment. I arrived around 3:30 to visit, and she was sound asleep. The nurse had given her medicine for pain. Marilyn seemed okay, and for that I was thankful. I left for home and told the nurse I would be back later.

I returned around 5:10. Marilyn was in her wheelchair in the dining room waiting for dinner. I tried to wake her but got little to no response. I sat down and continued talking to her, trying to get her to open her eyes. The pain medication she was given earlier still made her drowsy.

About 5:45 her food tray was served, and I told the server I would feed her. I gave her a sip of chocolate milk, which comes with every meal, just to awaken her taste buds. She responded, so I fed her. She stared at me as though she was trying to figure out who this person was. Then, all of a sudden, she grabbed my arm with both hands and pulled it to her chest and hugged it. She did not want to let me go. Tears came to my eyes as she slowly pulled my hand to her lips and kissed it. Marilyn had expressed her love to me at this moment in time without a word being spoken. She released my arm after her kiss.

I continued feeding her, and after she was finished, I pushed her wheelchair to the TV area of the facility where she fell asleep.

On Saturday, September 15, I arrived at the nursing facility around 12:15 and went to the dining room to search for Marilyn. She was in her wheelchair at a table waiting for lunch. I slowly approached the front of her wheelchair without saying a word. I wanted to see what her response would be.

When she felt my presence, she looked up at me, and with outstretched arms hugged and kissed me. Then she said, "I miss you!"

My response was the same. How much sadness can be brought to bear on hearts already stricken with grief? At this moment, she had expressed her warm, tender, and heartfelt feelings for me.

The next day I arrived at the nursing home around noon and went to the dining room to see if Marilyn was there. The nurse said she was taking a shower. I knew she would be cold after her shower, so I got her cap, pillow, and blanket to put on her when she arrived in the dining room. When the attendant brought her to the table where I fed her lunch, I put the cap on and the pillow behind her head.

I leaned down to give her a kiss and she said, "Thank you for taking care of me." Then she began crying. Tears filled my eyes.

My assessment of Marilyn's condition as her husband had

been ongoing. Each day was different from the previous day. She had some good days and some not so good. There were days when she had much anxiety. She constantly picked at her clothes. Sometimes she tried to get out of her wheelchair and was subject to falling on the floor.

Today, being Valentine's Day, when I woke this morning, I opened our dresser. In one drawer I found all those Valentine cards Marilyn kept over the years. I remembered the selection of cards, candies, flowers, and gifts that were exchanged expressing our love and thankfulness to each other. Because of Marilyn's condition and safety issues, my Valentine's gift to her today was a small teddy bear that said, "I Love You!"

Marilyn was only able to speak a few words that could be understood. Crying seemed to be her way to express that her head was hurting or there was pain in other parts of her body. Other times when she was crying, it was her way of communicating to me through expressions. The feelings were such that we had become as one in understanding each other. When I looked into her eyes and she looked directly into mine, neither of us speaking, the communication was in each of the other's thoughts. Today she looked into my eyes crying tears that flowed down her cheek. She was telling me she was dying but didn't want to leave me. Both of us shed many tears as I leaned down for her to kiss me. Then she left my presence with a faraway stare, looking into that other world. The stares may last fifteen to thirty seconds at a time before returning to the present surroundings. The medical experts told me this was a natural occurrence when one prepares to make the transition from this earthly life to that eternal life.

The dying process for Alzheimer's patients is a slow, gradual, methodical process. It was one that I had witnessed and been part of on a daily basis for the past ten months. We all have to face death alone, but at the time of death, we shouldn't be alone. It was my hope that I could be with Marilyn to hold her hand at the time of her passing.

Thursday, February 21, 2019

Today, more noticeable changes occurred in Marilyn's eating and sleeping habits. Her sleeping and eating in the past have fluctuated. Some days she might eat a good breakfast and then sleep through lunch. Then she would wake for dinner and eat all her meal. Other times she might eat her lunch and sleep through dinner. This was her pattern in the past. Today, she still ate the pureed foods but was eating less and less of them. She preferred foods that were liquids, such as soups, water, tea, shakes, and other drinks thickened with honey because they were less likely to go down the wrong passageway and cause her to choke.

I met with the hospice nurse today. She seemed puzzled as to why I spent so much time at the facility. Her concern was about my physical health and well-being.

The nurse's question to me was, "How are you going to deal with the loss when it comes?"

My answer was, "I don't know!"

I took care of Marilyn all those years she was in good health. I was now searching deep within to find the strength and courage to prepare myself for her being absent from my life. The nurse suggested I start thinking of a hobby or something to occupy my time. I can only say, as of now, Marilyn has been my life and my love as I have been hers. When she leaves my presence to enter that eternal world, part of me would accompany her on that journey.

Our Testimony

As I reflect on our spiritual journey, the Bible was used as our roadmap of faith to guide us through our forty-eight-year marriage. The early goal we set for ourselves was to help each other get to heaven when our life is completed on earth.

There were many great biblical lessons we learned throughout our marriage. Lessons, such as those recorded in chapters 5–7 of Matthew spoken by Jesus, taught with compassion and love, helped guide us through this sin-laden world. Yet Marilyn and I never led perfect lives, and we never claimed to be perfect. However, we followed Jesus, the one who forgave our sins, was perfect in living his life, and set the perfect example for all to follow. Our testimony of faith lay in the spoken words of Jesus, words spoken through his personal ministry, in predicting his death, in words spoken that concluded in his death, and words spoken of his resurrection prior to his death.

One lesson we learned that has stood the test of time as having the most and lasting impact on our hearts and lives was spoken by the Master Teacher in predicting his death. Jesus compared himself to a grain of wheat, saying, "Very truly I tell you, unless a kernel of wheat falls to the ground and dies, it remains only a single seed. But if it dies, it produces many seeds" (John 12:24 NIV)[3]. By comparing himself figuratively to a wheat seed, our eyes were opened to the message being taught. He must die as a seed and be planted in the ground (tomb) to be raised at the dawning of light on day three to produce more seeds in his likeness.

Over the years attending church, we sang an old gospel song many times. The lyrics were by Isaac Watts, and the line I found most meaningful was, "At the cross, at the cross where I first saw the light." The song, the message, and the love of the

Savior best relate to our understanding from the messenger, who delivered in the first-century AD the greatest sermon ever spoken using the cross as his podium and recorded in all four gospels.

In reading of Jesus's death in the gospels, the physical pain he endured could only be imagined. Combined with the mental torture of his father leaving him from 9:00 a.m. to 3:00 p.m. while suspended between heaven and earth is unimaginable. Though human in form just as we are, yet divine in character, he could not understand why his father had forsaken him.

God knew his son was the only one who could stand alone though sinless himself, yet divinely forsaken with the sins of the world crucified to him. Therefore, God forsook his one Son so he would not forsake Marilyn, myself, and his other sons and daughters.

The mystery of how Satan would be defeated was hidden with God "before the ages began" (1 Corinthians 2:7-8, New King James Version).[4] Whereas that mystery is now known in Jesus who spoke in the climax of his sermon those concluding words, "It is finished" (John 19:30, NKJV).[5] It was in those words that he summed up his mission on earth while waiting on death. In that moment, Satan knew his time had just expired. His head was bruised (see Genesis 3:15 for more information) and his destiny sealed.

Then Jesus "cried out again with a loud voice and yielded up his spirit" (Matthew 27:50-51, NKJV)[6]. It was "that through death he might destroy him who had the power of death, that is the devil" (Hebrews 2: 14, NKJV).[7] God's "eternal purpose" (Ephesians 3:11, NKJV)[8] was accomplished in the defeat of Satan through his son Jesus. Although Jesus died alone, we never felt alone because our faith is in "Emmanuel, which being interpreted is, God with us" (Matthew 1:23b, King James Version).[9] The message of the cross has revealed to us the love of God for mankind through his son Jesus. Though crucified and risen two thousand years ago, in remembrance his blood is still flowing, pouring out in love, a savior born to be humble, lived to love, served to die, and died in forgiveness!

The question we asked ourselves was this: Why did God send his son Jesus to earth to suffer at the hands of mankind a life of humiliation, rejection, and death even though in prophecy his coming as the Messiah had been looked for and awaited with great anticipation long before he arrived (See Isaiah 53 for more information)?

The answer: God loves his children equal to his son Jesus and has made them "heirs—heirs of God and co- heirs with Christ"(Romans 8:17, NIV).[10] Our faith, hope, and trust has been placed in God's wisdom, which is eternal (See 1 Corinthians 2:1-16 for more information)[11].

Although our physical walk together since October 4, 1970, was coming to an end, our spiritual goal to help each other get to heaven was getting closer for Marilyn to achieve. Since 2015, the year she was diagnosed with Alzheimer's, the progression through stages, though slow, was predictable in her experiencing misplacing things around the house, having to give up driving our car, not being able to write checks, and being lost in Walmart. The disease reversed her mind to that of a three-year-old child. As terrible as this may seem, the disease still could not take away her spiritual life with Jesus.

We thank you, God, for your wisdom which was "ordained before the ages for our glory" (1 Corinthians 2:7, NKJV)[12] in the giving of your Son Jesus, who has adopted us to be his children as well as all others who hear his voice calling them for adoption (See Romans 8:14-17 for more information).[13] This is the Savior who Marilyn and I worshiped and served, not because we were free to worship him but because we love him. He has proclaimed freedom to us and all his children in his death and set us free, "free from the law of sin and death" (Romans 8:2, NKJV).[14] The message of the cross influenced the decisions we made in marriage and raising our family.

Reflections

My reflection on my life and the choices that were made was that some were bad, a few I would like to have changed, while others were good.

The two choices I never regretted were when I obeyed the gospel of Christ and became a Christian, and when I asked Marilyn to marry me. When she said yes, that was the second blessed day of my life. Those two choices have had a lasting effect on how I conducted my life. When she came to the gym in Magazine forty-eight years ago, I didn't know at the time nor did I realize at the time that this stranger was going to be my lifelong partner. Basketball didn't seem as important as previously thought when she walked through those double doors to the gym at three o'clock on October 4, 1970.

Our time was about to begin. I will always believe that prayers provided an opportunity for our meeting. We were both beginning our careers as educators. The opportunity presented us with choices to make. I would never recommend to anyone after only two months of dating to get married. That being said, the question I ask myself is what was going on between us for those few short moments? Neither of us tried to make a sales pitch to the other on how great we were at anything. We were in observation mode. What was outwardly seen was inwardly felt. We were in a search for words. Silence dominated the conversation. That's when I felt a need to join in the scrimmage to gather my thoughts and get my mind back to basketball. There was something intervening or occurring in our lives that words just can't explain!

Alzheimer's is a disease that is nondiscriminatory in nature. The disease can infiltrate the mind of anyone, no matter how rich or poor. It is a silent killer that chips away at the mental functions of the brain until the memory is gone. It makes no difference which class you belong to; everyone is vulnerable to a disease that has no boundaries. It is unpredictable on a daily basis. One day my wife seemed to recognize me as her husband; the next day there seemed to be no difference between me and one of the attendants working at the facility. It was like the disease controlled her thought processes and what would be remembered and spoken daily.

When my wife entered the nursing home, I was told she would have moments of expressing her feelings to me in the form of hugs and kisses. Now these moments were becoming less frequent. The time was near for the final page of her life to be closed.

How do you close a chapter in one's life that has not been lived? A life that should still have years of productivity. The disease robbed her of precious years she would have spent with her husband, family, and friends celebrating the joy of Christmas, Thanksgiving, birthdays, anniversaries, and all the other holidays and everything else in between.

It is believed American clergyman George Washington Burnap once said the key to happiness is to have something to do, something to hope for, and someone to love. Our professions provided us with our livelihood. Our hope was attained through faith in Jesus Christ as the Son of God, followed by a systemic study of God's word. This helped us make informed decisions and practical applications to our lives and gave us eternal hope when this life is over. Our love and commitment to each other made our lives rich, full of inward peace, joy, happiness, and love. Marilyn and I were blessed to share all these attributes.

What more can be said of this physical life full of disappointments, sadness, and sorrow than to say we laughed, cried, and loved each other. There would be a void of her physical presence, but the memory of Marilyn and her life will forever remain. As her husband, I cannot think of a greater tribute to this woman who has shared her life with me than is recorded in Proverbs 31:11–12: "The heart of her husband safely trusts her. She does him good and not evil all the days of her life."

Tuesday, August 6, 2019

I arrived at the nursing home around 12:20. Lunch was being served. Marilyn was already at the table where I usually fed her, though today seemed to have a different feeling. I felt her hands and feet. They were cold though covered with a blanket. I couldn't get her to wake up. She had slept through lunch before, so I wasn't alarmed. I asked an aide if she ate breakfast. The aide who fed her breakfast said she would not eat. This was unusual. She always ate her breakfast.

Now the time was 1:20, and she was still unresponsive, so I decided to leave. After running a few errands, I stopped at a restaurant for lunch around 3:20. I received a call from the hospice nurse stating that mottling was starting to occur. (Mottling is caused by the heart no longer being able to pump blood effectively throughout the body.) The nurse informed me she would be moved to a private room because she was now entering the last stage of the disease.

Leslie, Rachel, and Myra, our granddaughter, gathered to visit. I decided to stay the night in the twin bed next to

Marilyn's. After the family left, I spent time with Marilyn in prayer and reading about those beautiful mansions described by Jesus in John 14:1–31. The reading helped me understand where Marilyn would be spending eternity.

Thursday, August 8

The time was after midnight. I was asleep on a bed beside Marilyn's bed. I woke to the sound of the door opening. Two nurses came in the room to give care to her. She was awake as well. Marilyn was trying to talk, but her words were not understood. They began turning her on her side, checking her vital signs. I observed some extra attention given, separate and apart from their professional duties, such as caressing her head, kissing her on the cheek, and even shedding a tear.

I said, "I see something in the care you're providing not associated with your professional training."

One stated that in her eight years of professional service, there had only been a few that stirred her emotions as Marilyn had in offering care.

The other nurse said she grew close to Marilyn by singing "Fa, la, la, la" and then Marilyn responded by singing, "La, la, la, la, la."

I stated, "Marilyn has those qualities of character like kindness, gentleness, and patience that I noticed when we first met."

The students she taught responded in kind to those qualities with respect. In life, we meet many people apart from family members of whom friendships are made. Some we make at work, some are friends with whom we confide, and then there are those few who will be remembered who possess those personal qualities that touch our hearts and lives by their presence. Marilyn was one of those rare friends and my wife who has made a difference in my life and in the lives of those who knew her.

Friday, August 9

Marilyn slept peacefully through Thursday night. The nurse informed me her pulse was getting weaker.

Wednesday, August 14

I had a dentist appointment that morning at nine that included a cleaning and a filling, followed with two teeth being extracted. While waiting on the effect of numbness caused by Novocain to complete the extractions, I received a call from the hospice nurse around 11:10. She said Marilyn had begun the "process of dying." She further said, "It may be hours or days, but the process has now started."

After the dentist completed his work, I left the office with a swollen jaw and gums filled with gauze pads. I arrived at the nursing home around 11:30. She was resting with eyes closed.

Thursday, August 15

Marilyn was awake when breakfast was served, yet she wouldn't eat. She was making noises and frowning. She seemed uncomfortable. Perhaps she felt small amounts of pain. I sent for the nurse. She gave her a dose of morphine and Ativan to calm her down and relieve the pain. She was no longer eating or accepting liquids. She choked and coughed up almost everything placed in her mouth.

Friday, August 16, 2019

The day began with breakfast being served around 7:00. Marilyn was asleep. The aide tried to wake her to eat, but no response. Marilyn had stopped eating. The time had come to reserve her energy to make that transition from this physical world to that unseen world.

She briefly opened her eyes a couple of times this morning. When she did, Rachel and I leaned in to kiss her cheek and to receive a kiss. Then she fell asleep. Rachel and I decided to go eat lunch at a restaurant located not far from the nursing home.

After lunch, we went back to Marilyn's room. Rachel had some computer work to complete, so I pulled up a chair by Marilyn's bed and held her hand. She awoke around 3:00. When she did, Rachel and I both leaned to her lips and received a kiss. This was her goodbye kiss. Then she closed her eyes and fell asleep.

I decided to lie on the twin bed next to Marilyn's, but before lying down, I emptied my pockets of change that I'd received after paying at the restaurant. As usual, I looked at the dates on the coins, especially pennies because the copper value in older pennies is worth more than the actual face value of the coin itself. One of the pennies was dated 1970, the year we were married. The other penny was dated 1968, the year my prayers began in searching for a mate. Coincidence? Perhaps. Though insignificant as it may seem, those two pennies would have gone overlooked if I had not looked at the dates on those coins. Was a Higher Power speaking to me as well as reminding me that my prayers were received in 1968, answered when we met on October 4, 1970, and a blessing for the forty-eight years that followed?

The pennies from my pocket on August 16, 2016. (Photograph by Johnny Cogburn)

After a short nap, Rachel woke me around 4:00 because Marilyn was awake, and she was staring at me. I took her hand and moved closer. With our eyes focused on each other, she was communicating her love for me and grieving for leaving me. Help she was wanting, yet help I could not give.

Closed Door

What questions would I ask if only I could? *Where is the door? The door is closed! Will it be opened? Who will open the door for me? I no longer have the strength to open the door myself! I see a ray of light on the other side of the door! Yet who will open the door for me? The light is becoming more radiant as I speak. The door is slightly opened, but not enough to walk through! Who will open the door for me? My child, there will be a time when the door will open on its own; the time has not yet arrived. Be patient, stand, and wait.*

I continued to hold her hand throughout this process, but what was I to do? A Bible quote came to mind spoken by Jesus, saying, "I am the resurrection and the life. He who believes in me, though he may die, he shall live"(John 11:25, NKJV).[15]

I have observed and lived through the dying process with my wife since 2015, the year she was diagnosed with Alzheimer's. She now has entered the perimeter of death, not the core of death but the circumference of death lasting forty-five minutes as Rachel, Matt, Leslie, Myra, and I listened to those chilling sounds as our loved one experienced the cruelty of death as it slowly approached. Then at 4:45, morphine was given, and Marilyn passed into eternity.

Opened Door

My door has now opened; time for me has run its course. I can now walk through the door that once was previously closed. The ray of light shines bright, brighter than ever before, and the presence of God is eternal. Time here will be no more for the glory of God is forever. He is behind the door. I can only hope to see you on the other side of the door. May all who hear and read know the splendor behind the door. Oh! Such beauty is indescribable and for all mankind to see.

So prepare yourself for God's glory and come follow me. In time your door will open for the radiance described above. Just prepare yourself for his presence and be patient, stand and wait.

The End of Our Life Journey

As she breathed her last, a quaint yet noticeable sound came from her mouth as her spirit left her body. At that moment, I said, "Soar on wings of eagles, Marilyn." I then closed those beautiful eyes of hers with my fingers as "death is swallowed up in victory" (1 Corinthians 15:54b, NKJV).[16]

Today, August 16, at 4:45 p.m., Marilyn left my presence and the world she once knew to enter that divine world where the tears from her beautiful eyes will be wiped away by Jesus (see Revelation 21:4 for more information)[17] who is "the author and finisher of our faith," (Hebrews 12:2a, NKJV)[18] where peace is found in him who made salvation possible in his death on the cross (see John 16:33 for more information).[19]

It is our prayer for those in reading from the Holy Scripture that their faith will guide them in finding that priceless, treasured, pearl through prayer, discernment, and the understanding of God's word (see Proverbs 2:4 and Matthew 13:45-46 for more information).[20] I will always think of Marilyn as that helpmate whom God gave to me as a gift for companionship to watch over, take care of, and cherish for a few years.

Now that gift was returned to the Giver as she took her place in her new home on high with the redeemed of past ages in a world that has no end. My prayer is that our life story will touch lives, serve purposes, and be blessed by the omnipotent hand of God.

We reached the conclusion of the journey of our lives, at least our lives as we currently knew them. Our story became your story with all the heartaches, disappointments, sadness, and sorrows of this world. As I attempted to bring closure, my thoughts traveled back to my childhood days and a way of life that was long forgotten in time. Future generations can only imagine what it would be like on a Saturday evening when your entertainment consisted of reading Bible stories by the light of a coal oil lamp, popping popcorn over an open fire, and listening to others tell stories of their life adventures without being interrupted by television or internet usage.

The final prayer of closing thoughts is written in letters, one from Marilyn to Johnny and one from Johnny to Marilyn.

> To my dear husband, Johnny,
>
> Where to begin? Words cannot express my feelings of love I have for you. The years were spent too fast. They seem like only yesterday. My memory of the shared times together will never be forgotten. Although I am not able to write this letter in person, my thoughts can be expressed through the one who was in my dreams before I knew him, the one who has always had my life, my love, my heart, and my trust. When I first saw you in the gym at Magazine, I immediately knew there was something special about our meeting

that words cannot describe. The eye contact, facial expressions, the absence of mind, and the emptiness of thought that were all present and happened within a five-minute period. At that moment I had a feeling you were the one for me. Let's just call it a woman's intuition. When you asked me to marry you, there were no hesitating moments or thoughts on my part. I just wanted to be near you and become your life. The years we had together were wonderful. You treated me with kindness and respect all throughout our marriage. You have always looked out for our family's best interest.

The years that I spent in public education were enjoyable. Many friends were made, and many students were taught. Our retirement years spent in Dardanelle in the home you built for me went fast. The simple times we spent just enjoying each other's company will always be remembered along with the quiet times we spent watching the flames and feeling the warmth of the open fire. My time on earth since we were married has been devoted to our family and making your life pleasant and happy. Our life together could have only been duplicated in the heavenly realm. My today and tomorrows have become brighter because you were there for me. I want to thank you for the support and daily care you gave me during my stay in the nursing home. I have to make this final walk without you being by my side, but your spiritual presence will accompany me when it's time for me to cross to the other side. Tell Shelly, Leslie, and Rachel goodbye with my love for them.

To Myra, my lovely granddaughter, my memory of you will be cherished always. Work hard in school, guard your heart, be sweet, kind, and gentle, and place God first in your life. I will love you forever.

Johnny, I will look for you when it becomes time for you to take that walk yourself. I thank you, my husband, for loving me and for our life together.

Love always,
Marilyn

Dearest Marilyn,

This book has been a blessing for me to write my thoughts, thoughts that are still romancing you though only in memory of the woman who opened the door to my heart forty-eight years ago. Also, in memory of a mother who loved and wanted the best for her daughters; a grandmother who loved her granddaughter; and a wife who gave her love and the best years of her life to me.

My thoughts are summed up in this poem, "Lost to Time":

My heart has been laid open in writing this book,

Speaking of times made simple to hearts and lives we've touched.

The happiness of times spent together, and the loneliness of times spent apart.

A book of pages never written, pages that never were turned, days, months, and years.

Dreams that never occurred.

As time passes, I will think of those simple times and places in our lives when we were young, when our future was only limited by our thoughts. After forty-eight years, seven months, and sixteen days of marriage, there is something that I want to say to you one more time at the close of our life together. Those memories of you will forever be frozen in time, in times spent together in the giving and taking of love. If only again you could hear my voice speak those tender, affectionate words of love to you, to you, my chosen words would be, "I love you, Marilyn."

Your loving husband,

Johnny

About the Author

Photograph by Jeremy Cowart.

Johnny Lee Cogburn lives in Fayetteville, Arkansas, near his three daughters. He graduated from the University of Central Arkansas and had a twenty-four-year coaching and teaching career in public schools. Since retirement, he devoted his time to his wife, Marilyn, and now his grandkids. Johnny enjoys cooking and likes to walk, cycle, and hike to stay fit.

CPSIA information can be obtained
at www.ICGtesting.com
Printed in the USA
LVHW091729220921
698472LV00007B/125